WOMEN
COMPOSERS

WOMEN COMPOSERS

The Lost Tradition Found

DIANE PEACOCK JEZIC

Foreword by Elizabeth Wood

THE FEMINIST PRESS
at The City University of New York
New York

© 1988 by Diane Peacock Jezic
Foreword © 1988 by Elizabeth Wood
All rights reserved.
Printed in USA
91 90 89 88 5 4 3 2 1
Published 1988 by The Feminist Press at The City University of New York,
311 East 94 Street, New York, NY, 10128
Distributed by The Talman Company, 150 Fifth Avenue,
New York, NY 10011

Permission acknowledgments begin on page 249.

Library of Congress Cataloging-in-Publication Data
Jezic, Diane.
Women composers.
Bibliography: p.
1. Women composers.   I. Title
ML390.J37 1988   780'.92'2 [B]   88-31052
ISBN 0-935312-94-3
ISBN 0-935312-95-1 (pbk.)

This publication is made possible, in part, by public funds from
the New York State Council on the Arts.

The musical score reproduced on the cover is from *Trio* for
tenor saxaphone, piano, and percussion (1982) by Edith Boroff.
It is used by permission of the composer.

Text design by Melodie Wertelet

To my mother, Mary Peacock, the composer who long ago inspired me, to my husband, Dragan Jezic, who supported me, to my children, Andrew and Tamara, who encouraged me, and to the memory of my loving father, Arthur Peacock

Contents

PART TWO
The Classical Period

PART THREE
The Romantic Period—Songs

PART FOUR
The Romantic Period and
Early Twentieth Century—Instrumental Music

PART FIVE
Six Living U.S. Composers

Foreword

Elizabeth Wood

In 1983 Ellen Taaffe Zwilich, one of the featured composers in this book, was awarded the Pulitzer Prize in Music, the first American woman to be so honored. She remarked at the time, "I hope this is encouragement for other women. It's kind of a good sign for the world. We're not that far away from the days when orchestras resisted having women players. I'd like to think I won for my piece, not as a symbol. But I don't mind being a positive symbol" (*New York Times,* Wednesday, May 4, 1983).

As we proceed to unearth the facts of women's history, we sometimes take for granted the more recent advances in women's status. Now women can join professional orchestras, and conduct them, and hear them play women's compositions, if too few and too infrequently. Recordings, editions, and commissions of women's music have multiplied; women music teachers have gained academic jobs; a scholarly literature of women's music has sprouted. Women composers have become more visible, more accomplished, and more numerous.

Yet their survival is not guaranteed. So many of our musical forebears, as this book reveals, disappeared from music history and from memory. The work of the happy few who are represented here—women of uncommon talent and determination—has survived because of two contributing factors: the availability to them of essential social and economic conditions to sustain creative work; and their own courage and will in over-coming psychological barriers to creative expression.

The following biographies tell us, first, that many of these women enjoyed the advantages of birth or marriage to a musical family, and of a technical and theoretical education; they acquired performance experience and publishers and financial sponsorship. Some made their music at home; others in women's communities such as nunneries and orphanages where music making was part of daily life; and many more expanded their public, professional careers as singers or instrumentalists in the European courts and salons into successful composing careers.

Second, given opportunities, even choices, in making their careers in music, women came up against a set of attitudes that threatened to silence and defeat them: a persistent sneer of patronage, tokenism, and trivialization that pronounced women fragile; that domesticated women's work; that kept women out of professions, out of history books, and out of positions, and even genres, of prestige and power. Only in this century have such attitudes and marginal positions begun radically—not merely symbolically—to change.

As long ago as 1902, the British composer and feminist Ethel Smyth remarked: "I must fight [for my work] because I want women to turn their minds to big and difficult jobs; not just to go on hugging the shore, afraid to put out to sea. I am an explorer who believes supremely in the advantages of this bit of pioneering" (Ethel Smyth, *What Happened Next* [London: Longmans, Green and Co., 1940], 210). Since composers sail into difficult waters with courage and perseverance, surely it's time that teachers and students do their "bit of pioneering" as well.

Those of us who teach music history, theory, and composition, and have occasional opportunities to create specialist courses on women in music, must now do all we can to integrate music by women into the general music curriculum and into texts which have consistently left women out, or at best have tacked them on as a last-minute, lip-service coda, to the end of an Introduction to Music survey.

Those of us working in the interdisciplinary programs of women's studies might begin to include music among the arts and accomplishments of women's history and culture, and give our students the chance to meet musicians whose lives and works are exemplary models—not merely symbols—of women's contributions both to music's traditions and also to the ongoing process of cultural change.

The task of "putting out to sea" has been tricky up to now because knowledge has been fragmentary, surviving sources are scattered, and the cost and time involved in collating materials is considerable. In nautical terms, we have lacked the necessary charts and soundings. Now Diane Jezic, with The Feminist Press at The City University of New York, has equipped us for the journey. Here is a musical map of selected women composers, assembled in a lucid, informal, well-organized way, and thoughtfully rigged with navigational aids, to help us survey more deeply, and beyond if we so desire, the story of women's music. Bon voyage!

Preface

Recent years have seen a rapid growth in feminist scholarship by and about women in music. Although course offerings in both women's studies and music programs have proliferated, publication of accessible literature about women composers for the general reader and student has lagged behind the scholarship. Those who wish to study women creators in the art of music have had to search for and collect scattered texts, and this effort has been compounded by the need to also discover and co-ordinate recordings of women's compositions, an essential element in learning about any composer's work.

The lack of available, accessible information and recordings became clear to me in the spring of 1985, when I surveyed fourteen music appreciation textbooks to determine the extent of their inclusion of women composers. The dismaying results, summarized in appendix 1, convinced me of the need to write this book. As late as 1985—and the situation has not changed much since then—three leading textbooks made absolutely no mention of any women composers, and only one text published between 1980 and 1985 offered any pieces by women in its accompanying recordings. I decided it was time to set the record straight.

Women Composers: The Lost Tradition Found is a guide to the lives and works of twenty-five composers of Western art music from the eleventh century to the present. The composers come from both Western Europe and the United States and are presented chronologically in five traditional music history periods. Each chapter is devoted to a single composer and includes a biographical summary, a discussion of the composer's life and work, an analysis of from one to four of her compositions, a selected list of her compositions, and a selected bibliography and discography for further reference. Discussion centers on the notable contributions and special life situations of the composer, how her music fits (or does not fit) into traditional music history, how it relates to or may have been influenced by contemporary male composers, and the socio-economic conditions that made composing possible for her.

The composers and the musical examples were selected with three goals in mind: (1) to represent the major periods and genres of music history; (2) to represent the best of what women have composed in those genres typically associated with them, namely songs, piano pieces, and small chamber music works, usually featuring string instruments, flute, and/or piano; and (3) to present some nonstereotypical genres, especially instrumental music, or excerpts from the larger genres usually associated with men (opera, cantata, the nonet), to dispel the myth that women couldn't compose in these areas. A balance was also sought between vocal and instrumental music.

The material in this book is arranged to accommodate the needs of teachers and students in a variety of music and women's studies courses. Integration of the study of women into traditional music history courses, for example, is facilitated by the presentation of material chronologically and by period, and by the discussion of women in relation to well-known and lesser known male contemporaries. Since women throughout history have composed many art songs, this is reflected in the highlighted compositions, making the book especially useful in vocal literature courses. Similarly, material is conveniently separated into historical units for period courses on Baroque, Classical, or Romantic music, or courses on twentieth-century music. A course on U.S. music could refer to those seven U.S. women included—Amy Beach and the six living composers of this century. A separate course on Women in Music can be built around this text as a whole.

The material can also be adapted for various women's studies courses. The texts to the vocal music, in combination with the biographical discussions, offer a framework for discussion of how the choice and setting of a text may have been influenced by these women's lives or a female aesthetic.

The Introduction discusses the major issues concerning the study of women composers, namely the historical representation of women in music history, the question of the presence of a feminine aesthetic in

Western art music, and problems inherent in the teaching of musicology (problems that adversely affect the incorporation of women composers into the music canon).

These twenty-five chapters represent only a sampling of women composers' activity in the last thousand years. Appendixes 2 through 6 provide supplementary information about the women featured here and many others. Appendix 2 provides the names and addresses of record companies that feature works by women; appendix 3 provides a chart of the styles and genres of over fifty women composers along with their male contemporaries from 850 through the 1940's; appendix 4 lists additional twentieth-century women composers born after 1920 and their favored genres; appendix 5 presents a list of selected women conductors, the important supporting cast in musical performance; and appendix 6 presents the extensive list of works by women available from Leonarda Productions, a pioneer in the recording and distribution of women's music. A detailed selected bibliography directs the reader to more information in texts, scores, and discographies.

One of the key features of this book is that recordings of the thirty-eight highlighted compositions are readily available from one source. Two cassettes containing the compositions in the order in which they are presented in the book have been specially produced by Marnie Hall of Leonarda Productions. Because the opportunity to hear the works being studied is crucial, and because it is often difficult to obtain recordings of many works by women, the book and tapes were conceived together to provide two tools that can be easily coordinated. Information about obtaining the cassettes can be found in appendix 6.

I believe this book is unique not only because of its coordination with recordings, but also because of its adaptability to a wide variety of uses both inside and outside the classroom. Unlike the more specialized texts on women in music, this book assumes only that its readers will be interested in music or women or both, and therefore will enjoy, as much as I have, the finding of the lost tradition.

Special thanks are due the following people: Elaine Hedges, Professor of English and Women's studies at Towson State University, and Florence Howe, Publisher of The Feminist Press, who believed in this project from the beginning; Marnie Hall, President of Leonarda Productions, who has made the tapes that accompany this book available; several students in my Women in Music course at Towson State University, particularly Laurie Harper Blake, who helped me make the book more student-oriented; the Women's Studies faculty at Towson State University, particularly Sara Coulter and, again, Elaine Hedges, whose procurement of a substantial FIPSE grant enabled us to integrate the study of women into our courses; my sister, Marilyn Stranahan, who proofread an earlier version of the book; Janet Kozlay, for preparation of an early typescript; and my editor at The Feminist Press, Susannah Driver, and my copyeditor Linda Carbone for their diligent preparation of the manuscript.

Particular thanks are due Edith Borroff, Judith Zaimont, and Elizabeth Wood, pioneers in the field of women in music, whose unceasing encouragement, friendship, and inspiration have sustained me throughout this project. Grateful acknowledgment is also due the following scholars and pioneers in the field, without whose research this book could not have been written: Christine Ammer, Jane Bernstein, Adrienne Fried Block, Jane Bowers, James Briscoe, Marcia Citron, Aaron Cohen, Bea Friedland, Barbara Garvey Jackson, Mildred Denby Green, Miriam Stewart Green, Jane Weiner LePage, Carol Neuls-Bates, Jeannie Pool, Carolyn Raney, Nancy Reich, Judith Rosen, Léonie Rosenstiel, Eileen Southern, and Judith Tick.

Featured Compositions and Coordinated Tapes

Recordings of the musical works featured in this book are all available, in the order in which they are discussed in the text, on two cassettes specially produced by Leonarda Productions. The list below provides the cassettes' example numbers as well as the composers' names and composition titles. The tapes are available directly from Leonarda Productions, a non-profit, woman-run recording company and a leader in the movement to produce and promote music by women since 1979. Order information and the complete list of works by women available from Leonarda Productions are given in appendix 6.

EXAMPLE NO.	COMPOSER	WORK(S)
SIDE ONE	MEDIEVAL, BAROQUE, AND CLASSICAL PERIODS	
1	Hildegard of Bingen (1098–1179)	*Kyrie*
2	Francesca Caccini (1587–1640)	a) Selection from *La Liberazione di Ruggierio* b) Chi desia si saper,' "che cos" e amore
3	Barbara Strozzi (1619–1644)	*Tradimento!*
4	Isabella Leonarda (1620–1704)	*Kyrie* from Mass op. 18
5	Elisabeth-Claude Jacquet de la Guerre (1666–1729)	a) Prelude from *Samson* b) *Tempete* from *Le Sommeil d'Ulisse*
6	Anna Amalia, Princess of Prussia (1723–1787)	*Regimental March*
7	Anna Amalia, Duchess of Saxe-Weimar (1739–1807)	Selections from *Erwin und Elmire*
8	Maria Theresia von Paradis (1759–1824)	*Sicilienne* for cello and piano
SIDE TWO	ROMANTIC LIEDER (SONGS)	
9	Louise Reichardt (1779–1826)	a) *Heir liegt ein Spielmann* b) *Betteley der Vögel*
10	Fanny Mendelssohn Hensel (1805–1847)	a) *Nachtwanderer* b) *Warum sind denn die Rosen so blass?* c) *Morgenständchen*

Introduction

The lives of the composers discussed in the twenty-five chapters that follow span a period of nearly nine hundred years. But regardless of whether the composer lived in the medieval period or the twentieth century, certain conditions peculiar to the discipline of music have proven necessary for sustaining her composing career. These include a specialized music education, a publisher or a music copyist, performances of works, an audience, and some degree of acceptance and/or encouragement of women working in a male-dominated field. In the case of twentieth-century women, publicity and/or reviews, recordings, radio broadcasts, public relations agents, grants, commissions, and financial backing and/or university affiliation are also necessary.

Before the twentieth century, if women creating music were to be recognized, they had to have been born into a musical family or grown up in the presence of royalty or in a family with court or patron affiliation; and/or they had to work in an all-female environment, such as in religious convents or the all-female Venetian conservatories. Without these advantages or prerequisites, very few, if any, musical women could hope to become composers. Even though a musical education became available to certain privileged women of the nineteenth century, it was

1

not until the twentieth century that a musical education became a possibility for middle-class women.

In addition to these requirements, many of the historical composers shared in common being first a performer, usually a singer or a pianist, who became well known for her virtuosity and performing skills before being accepted as a composer; performing or having her works performed in the private sphere such as home concerts of vocal, piano, or chamber music; writing in the genres considered acceptable for females—keyboard or chamber ensembles, solo song, or vocal chamber works—which could be performed with a small number of people; and, when setting secular texts to music, preferring such "female subjects" as romantic love or the praise of nature.

Whether integrating these twenty-five women into traditional music history, women's studies courses, or separate courses on women in music, three questions must be addressed: (1) What opportunities did women have to compose, or how well were they represented in each period of music?; (2) Can one identify a feminine aesthetic in Western art music?; and (3) How can traditional musicology be redefined to reflect the accomplishments of so many gifted women composers? The following discussion of these three issues is offered as a context, or frame of reference, for students and teachers of music appreciation, music history, and women's studies.

Historical Representation

In the medieval period (from approximately 900 to 1400 A.D.), music making by women was centered in the convents. Singing the liturgy from morning to night, musician nuns could also compose their own chants, which doubtless became incorporated into the huge repertory of anonymous chants. The abbess Hildegard of Bingen is representative of this very favorable period for religious women composers.

There was also a tradition of secular music making, especially in France, from which women were not excluded. The troubadours and trouvères, whose songs were for the most part settings of courtly love poems, counted several women among their ranks, in particular Countess Beatrice of Dia (b. ca. 1160) and Maria of Ventadorn (b. ca. 1165). In fact, in the early part of the thirteenth century, when professional minstrels were required to register their names in Paris, the names of eight women appeared among the signatures.

During the early Renaissance (approximately 1450 to 1560), women had practically no opportunities to learn the theoretical skills necessary for composing in the complicated polyphonic styles of the period. They were excluded from participating in church services, with the exception of convent life, and they were excluded from the master-apprentice tradition of learning their craft. However, in the last half of the sixteenth century, Italian courts began to seek out and train young women singers, a few of whom also composed. Four Italian women are representative of this period: Maddalena Casulana (1540–1583), Tarquinia Molza (1542–1583), and the Aleotti sisters of Ferrara, Raffaela (b. 1570, d. after 1646) and Vittoria (b. 1575, d. after 1620).

During the Baroque period (approximately 1600 to 1750), women continued to be accepted, primarily as singers, where they received training and/or tutoring within musical families, courts, or the convents. The most successful composers of this time—Francesca Caccini, Barbara Strozzi, and Isabella Leonarda—wrote mostly vocal music. However, the renowned French harpsichordist-composer Elisabeth-Claude Jacquet de la Guerre wrote a substantial number of instrumental works along with cantatas, oratorios, and other vocal pieces.

During the Classical period (approximately 1750 to 1810), several women composers wrote in instrumental genres similar to those favored by Joseph Haydn and Wolfgang Mozart. Since these women tended to be solo keyboardists, piano concerti, sonatas, and chamber music featuring keyboard instruments, in addition to solo songs accompanied at the keyboard, were added to the repertoire of music composed by women. Much of this instrumental music was intended for domestic use by amateur musicians, a large group of whom were women, and as a result did not receive the attention garnered by works for professional performance, composed mainly by men.

During the Romantic period (approximately 1810 to 1900), opportunities for women composers increased as musical education became more accessible. With the opening of public, secular conservatories and with certain prestigious academies of music admitting women to classes, there emerged a sizable group of women composers who gained the confidence necessary to write in the larger genres of that period: grand opera, symphonies, concerti, symphonic poems, and extended solo sonatas. With few exceptions, this new breed of women composers gained prominence first as soloists or touring artists. Practically all of the women composers of the Romantic period worked in genres other than those involving their own particular solo or performing medium. Fanny Mendelssohn Hensel's and Clara Wieck Schumann's names may be familiar because they are included in music textbooks as wife or sister of the more famous male counterpart. But they were also composers in their own right, and there remains a substantial number of women composers of the nineteenth century whose names are unfamiliar.

The living U.S. composers present a contrast, not only in their style of composition and use of unusual genres but in their musical educations, with seemingly equal access with male composers to education, at least in the last half of this century. Today, most women composers are university-trained and are well represented in university faculties as teachers of singing, piano, pedagogy, music appreciation, and lower levels of music theory. However, it is still a rarity to find a female "composer-in-residence," a status enjoyed by many male faculty members.

It is significant, I think, that some of today's contemporary women composers, represented here by Ellen Zwilich, Judith Zaimont, and Barbara Kolb, do not actively seek college teaching jobs, the traditional haven for most composers of modern music. Instead they are making their way doing what they do best—composing—on commission from small and large performing organizations. Since 1983, with the awarding of the Pulitzer Prize in Music Composition to Ellen Zwilich, the professional world of music performance has begun to make a good faith effort to commission choral and instrumental works from these women.

Can One Define a Feminine Aesthetic in Western Art Music?

Two issues are raised by this question. The first involves the history of how women's music has been judged by standards imposed by male-dominated society, or affected by the strictures historically placed on women. The second involves the more subjective area of discerning a distinct feminine aesthetic in the kind of art music we are discussing.

Women composers' historical representation, as outlined above, chronicles an overwhelming emphasis on the woman performer, the singer or keyboardist who, once recognized as an accomplished performer, could venture into composing in those genres considered appropriate to her "place": art songs and piano pieces. Furthermore, with the advent of music criticism and music journalism in nineteenth-century Germany, "strong" instrumental music such as symphonies, concerti, and operas was considered masculine, and "sentimental or melodious" music was considered feminine. More active = masculine; more passive, more lyrical = feminine. Femininity in music was equated with beautiful melodies, refinement, and sensitivity. Vocal music was considered appropriate for women, since it manifested most clearly the above-named characteristics. But as far as instrumental music was concerned, harmony and counterpoint were often considered too intellectual, too logical for a woman to attempt. Apparently, she was supposed to rely on her feelings, which were supposed to produce inspired, singable melodies.

Up until the twentieth century, when women did compose in the more intellectual or "higher" forms, they were often viewed as bold and

daring, essentially betraying their feminine nature as defined by mainstream society. The highest praise a critic could offer a woman sympho-
nist was that she composed like a man. This placed women composers
in a double bind. When they composed in the genres accepted as feminine—songs, piano pieces, or salon music—they were doing what society
expected of them, but they were also perpetuating the myth of their
inability to work in larger, more abstract genres and forms. On the other
hand, when they did attempt to write in larger forms, especially absolute
music, they might be viewed as betraying their feminine identity. Is it
any wonder that with Goethe's image of the eternal feminine, coupled
with ideas about women's private sphere as opposed to men's public
sphere, most nineteenth-century women continued to write parlor songs
and sentimental keyboard music?

In their Introduction to *Women Making Music: The Western Art Tradition, 1150–1950,* Jane Bowers and Judith Tick discuss the detrimental
effects such gender-specific stereotypes have had on women composers.
Documenting the type of music criticism leveled at women composers,
they quote a German-American, Edward Naumann, in his *History of Music,* published in 1882: "all creative work is well-known as being the
exclusive work of men" (p. 8). Enough said.

In addressing the more subjective question of seeking a feminine aesthetic in art music, the nature of aesthetics should first be considered. If
aesthetics is defined as a response to the nature of beauty, art, or artistic
expression, then it involves personal valuations. Valuations are often the
result of experience, and women's collective experience is different from
men's.

An important issue here, one that is particularly subjective, is whether
one can suggest a feminine aesthetic in music composed without a text,
that is, *absolute music.* This is the area in which traditional musicologists
will invariably ask, "How good is that particular instrumental work?"
By this they mean, "Please compare this instrumental work with those
of her male contemporaries." By what barometer can one evaluate feminine absolute music, composed for instruments or instrumental ensemble?

Historically, women's lack of music experience or education has de-
prived many of the technical knowledge required for writing a decent
development section, for instance (as in first movements of string quartets, sonatas, concerti, or symphonies composed in classic traditional
form). And yet, it is entirely possible that, even if well educated, women
have not been as interested as their male contemporaries in displaying
how well they can craft musical phrases into fragmented, inverted, or
extended musical motives.

It is somewhat less problematic to seek a feminine aesthetic in music composed to a text. Since the choice of the poetry or libretto can be viewed as reflecting essential concerns of the composer, male or female, one might examine not only the nature of the text but any subtle reasons behind its choice.

Male and female composers of the Romantic period favored poetry that expressed such goals as romantic love or the love of nature. In some cases, the choice of art song text clearly pinpoints a feminine aesthetic similar to that of such well-known blues singers as Ma Rainey or Billie Holiday. In other cases, the choice of poetry for art songs by women may be strikingly similar to the glorification of nature or of romantic love, as seen in the Lieder of Franz Schubert or Robert Schumann. However, the romantic ideals of nationalism and hero worship so often favored by men composers are conspicuously missing from Romantic women composers' text settings.

The interested reader might consult volume ten of the journal *Heresies* for further discussion, pro and con, of whether there is a feminine aesthetic in music.

Toward a Redefined Musicology

As has been mentioned, the names of a few women composers have become known to the general music public because of their relation to famous men in history, for example, as wives, daughters, or favorite students. Because traditional musicology has tended to perpetuate the study of "the great masterpieces" composed by "the great masters," it has been musicians working in nontraditional disciplines (such as American music, black composers, or women's studies) who have begun to reexamine the nature of musicology.

We who have taught separate courses on women in music have been made aware of the difficulties in maintaining a strict musicological approach to the subject. Furthermore, the preparation and expectations of tradition-oriented music majors and nontradition-oriented women's studies majors are vastly different. The following story illustrates some of the problems involved in teaching women's studies students together with music majors, when one course on women in music lumps the two disciplines together.

Several years ago Nancy, the lone women's studies major in my Women in Music class of fifteen music majors, toward the end of the semester finally questioned, "Why are you just trying to fit the music of rediscovered women composers into a male-oriented, i.e., male-written history of music?" Unfortunately, the music students in the class couldn't sympathize with what she was asking.

A year later, the situation was reversed. Invited to lecture on women in music for the women's studies Culture and Creativity class, I adjusted my lecture and tapes accordingly. Susan, a music major, wanted to visit the class, until I told her what I would be talking about: the folk music of Joan Baez and Joni Mitchell, the suffrage and temperance songs of a bygone era, in addition to some historical composers of art songs. Susan decided to stay home.

In my own experience, I have encountered far more Susans than Nancys in the professional world of music. Unfortunately, the Susans have persisted in resisting what they perceive as a women's studies approach to studying music. What they don't know, yet, is that the best of the scholarship in women's studies seeks to raise those basic issues that any open-minded teacher has to face, regardless of what she or he is teaching. Whether one teaches voodoo songs or medieval chant, it is necessary to consider the context, and that is the first step toward a greater appreciation of what women's studies is all about.

In breaking down a preconceived hierarchical value system, and in offering different approaches to different experiences in people's lives, more sensitized students and teachers might ask the following questions in examining traditional musicology:

1. What really makes "good music"? Whose perception is counted? Is Mildred and Patty Smith Hill's "Happy Birthday" any less deserving of inclusion in the "greats" than Haydn's Sixty-ninth Symphony?
2. Isn't it reasonable to teach *music* instead of *composers,* i.e., the great masters? By teaching genres such as song, or any form of vocal music, or piano music, there is no end to the inclusion of musical examples by women (blacks, native Americans, native Africans, and so on).
3. How long must we honor the music hierarchies? Must long and complicated symphonies be the measure of a composer's worth?
4. What is so hallowed about the public concert hall? How long must the home, the church, the whole oral tradition remain second-class?
5. Shouldn't we approach any artwork from the universal point of view: "When, how, why, for what purpose, to express which feelings was the artwork created?"
6. What were the special circumstances surrounding women's lives that made them create the music they did?

Some new terminology must be added to traditional music history, if women are to receive their due attention: hegemony, hierarchy, social context, vernacular, the private sphere, iconography; and the concepts of class and race, as well as gender, must be incorporated. After all, in the words of my friend, the composer, musicologist, author, and teacher Edith Borroff, "Who could ever accuse you of not teaching great music if you include in your music course the Hill sisters 'Happy Birthday to You' or Effie Canning's 'Rock-a-bye Baby'?"

PART ONE

The Medieval and Baroque Periods

Hildegard of Bingen

(1098–1179)

Life in the Medieval Convents

Biographical Summary

1098	Born into a noble family which pledged this, their tenth child, to the service of God.
1106	Placed in convent in Disibodenberg, Germany.
1136	Becomes abbess of that convent.
1147	Moves, with eighteen nuns, to her own abbey at Rupertsberg, near Bingen. Here, her authority increases, as does her creative musical output.
1150	Begins collecting and illuminating the manuscripts of her many works for liturgical use in the convent.
1160–79	Travels along the Rhine preaching and teaching, even though it is forbidden for women.

As an abbess, composer, poet, mystic, teacher, consultant to popes and heads of state, and writer of visionary and scientific works, Hildegard's life has been documented over the centuries by religion and poetry scholars and fellow mystics. But only recently has some of her music been transcribed from medieval to traditional notation, thus facilitating more frequent performance of her works.

Several of her most significant compositions are extant, complete with original poetry and music. Most notable among these are the manuscripts to her *Symphonia harmoniae caelestium revelationum* (1150–60), a collection of seventy-seven "songs," as Hildegard referred to them, for liturgical use, and her *Ordo Virtutum* (1141–51), one of the earliest extant morality plays or liturgical dramas.

Integrating Hildegard into the Western tradition of sacred plainchant is not without its problems. Chronologically, she predates Leonin (ca. 1163–1190) of the St. Martial School by about twenty years, if one considers that Hildegard did not start writing down her liturgical songs until approximately 1141. She predates Perotin by a good half-century, if one sets 1200 as the approximate date of the Notre Dame School, as represented by Perotin. But Hildegard cannot be compared to either Leonin or Perotin.

Why? First and foremost is the fact that she composed mostly monophonic music in the form of sacred plainchant, for which she wrote original poetry. Although her music was intended for liturgical use, it is nevertheless strikingly original in its large melodic range and its avoidance of set melodic patterns and exact formula repetitions. But if one is pushed to assign Hildegard a place in traditional music history, she should perhaps be more appropriately compared to Notker Balbulus (ca. 840), monk of the Benedictine Abbey of St. Gall (Switzerland), whose book of musical sequences, *Liber Hymnorum,* also included original texts, employing mostly biblical and classical subjects. One could also stretch the literary comparison to include Adam of the Abbey of St. Victor, outside Paris, whose twelfth-century prose was likewise highly original, although still intended for liturgical use.

One last comparison of Hildegard to anything or anyone would necessarily have to include a description of monastic life in the Middle Ages, where singing was the order of the day. In fact, Hildegard's abbey at Bingen consisted of a community of about fifty women with trained voices, all of whom daily sang the seven offices of Matins, Lauds, Prime, Terce, Sext, None, and Vespers, plus the eucharistic liturgy. Quite a milieu for a composer! Indeed, the central task of a Benedictine nun or monk was to sing the liturgy, which must have required at least eight hours on a normal day, not to mention special feast days or other occasions.

Hildegard was particularly fortunate to have two devoted friends who helped her for over thirty years: Magister Volmar, who taught her Latin grammar construction, and a nun, Rikkarda, who assisted Hildegard in recording her visions.

Furthermore, the Benedictine order, from the seventh through the eleventh centuries, exerted considerable influence on the outside world. It not only provided the church with bishops and officials but also provided advisers and rulers in secular affairs. It wasn't until the rise of the urban university and the copying and illumination of books and manuscripts by lay persons that the Benedictines lost some of their power.

Soon after Hildegard's death in 1179, Popes Gregory IX (1227–41) and Innocent IV (1243–54) initiated the process of considering her for canonization. Although she was never proclaimed a saint, she was granted her own feast day, September 17. During her life, Hildegard was known not only for her music but for her prophecies and miracles. Referred to as "the Sybil of the Rhine," she was consulted by popes, emperors, kings, archbishops, and abbots, as she became increasingly involved, toward the end of her long life, in politics, teaching, and diplomacy.

Closely related to the Benedictine era, or rather to medieval monastic life in general, is the composer's belief in the complete abrogation of the self. Hildegard believed that every work she composed, every vision she recorded, every book she wrote, was the result of God speaking through her. The effects of such divine inspiration are evident in her mystically revealed, almost apocalyptic, texts. Although the following musical example is not representative of her vivid textual imagery, it is representative of her highly individual compositional style. The discussion below, as for all the musical examples in this book, refers to the recording available on cassettes LE3–4 from Leonarda Productions.

Musical Example
Kyrie

The texts of the five classic chants of the Ordinary of the Mass were more or less established by Hildegard's time: the Kyrie, Gloria, Credo, Sanctus, and Agnus Dei. As the first item of the mass, the text of the Kyrie is invariable: *Kyrie eleison; Christe eleison; Kyrie eleison.* ("Lord have mercy, Christ have mercy, Lord have mercy"). Although Hildegard follows the accepted form of three repetitions for each section (*aaa bbb àdà*), the melodic range she employs is much wider than that in conventional Gregorian chant. In fact, it encompasses more than an octave. Most unusual, also, is the feeling for the major mode, a melodic development that would not appear for at least three more centuries.

In order to contrast the middle section, *Christe eleison,* in this performance, the solo voice begins in a subdued dynamic level. This section is further identifiable by its contrastingly lower range. Like most Kyries, this one is highly melismatic, using many notes per text syllable.

What is interesting here is that this Kyrie is not part of a mass, and this was typical for nuns of the medieval period. There is no extant setting of the complete Ordinary of the mass by Hildegard. This Kyrie comes from her collection *Symphonia harmoniae caelestium revelationum* (1150–60).

Selected List of Works
Music

Ordo Virtutum (1141–51), a morality play with 85 songs
Symphonia harmoniae caelestium revelationum (1150–60), containing the poetry and music for:
    43 antiphons
    18 responds
    7 sequences
    4 hymns
    1 Kyrie
    1 allelujah
    and other miscellaneous items

Other

Scivias, a book of 26 divine revelations
Liber divororum operum (1163–70)
Liber vite meritorum (1158–63)
(Together the above form a trilogy of apocalyptic visions)
The Life of St. Disibod (1170–72)
The Life of St. Rupert (1172)
Meteria Medice, a book about medieval medicine

Selected Discography

Gesänge: Psallitte 242
O virga ac diadema, chorus: Columbia 80102
Sequenz an Maria: Psallitte 138/250937
Urbs aquaenis: Columbia 80102
Sequences and hymns: Hyperion A 66039

Selected Bibliography

Grant, Barbara. "Five Liturgical Songs by Hildegard von Bingen." *Signs: Journal of Women in Culture and Society* 5, no. 3 (1980).
Jeskalian, Barbara Jean. "Hildegard von Bingen." In *Historical Anthology of Music*

by Women, ed. James Briscoe. Bloomington, IN: Indiana University Press, 1987.

Neuls-Bates, Carol. "Life at a Twelfth-Century Benedictine Convent" and "Hildegard of Bingen: Abbess and Composer." In *Women in Music: An Anthology of Source Readings from the Middle Ages to the Present.* New York: Harper & Row, 1982.

The New Grove Dictionary of Music and Musicians, 1980 ed. S.v. "Hildegard of Bingen," by Jan Dent.

Yardley, Anne Bagnall. "Ful weel she soong the service dyvyne: The Cloistered Musician in the Middle Ages." In *Women Making Music: The Western Art Tradition, 1150–1950,* ed. Jane Bowers and Judith Tick. Chicago: University of Illinois Press, 1986.

Francesca Caccini

(1587–1640)

The Medici Court of Florence

Biographical Summary

ca. 1587	Born in Florence, the eldest daughter of composer Giulio Caccini and his wife, Lucia, a singer.
Early childhood	Studies singing, lute, harpsichord, and composition with her father; writes poetry in Latin and Tuscan.
1600	Performs in Peri's *Euridice* on occasion of Marie de Medici's wedding to Henry IV of France.
1604–05	Travels with her family, at the request of Marie de Medici, to court of King Henry IV in France.
1606	Begins composing canzonettas (texts by M. Buonarroti).
1607	Officially enters the service of the Medici court. Marries Giovanni Battista Signorini, poet and musician in Florentine court.
1614	Composes music for intermedios of comedies.
1615	Her *Ballo delle Zingare* is performed in Florence, the composer playing the role of the gypsy.
1616	Travels to Rome with Cardinal Medici and entourage.

1618	First publication, *Il Primo Libro,* dedicated to Cardinal Medici.
1618–23	Teaches singers in a school that she founded.
1619	Sets to music Buonarroti's play *La Fiera.*
1619–23	Court appearances with her two daughters.
1623	Highest paid singer at court.
1625	*La Liberazione di Ruggiero* performed in Florence for the visit of Polish Prince Sigismund.
1627	Stops collecting pay at Medici court; nothing further reported on her activities.

Virtuoso singer, composer, teacher, and skilled performer on the lute and harpsichord, Francesca Caccini enjoyed all the rights and privileges of being born into a famous musical family and of growing up in the resplendent Medici court in Florence. Taught principally by her father, Giulio Caccini (1546–1618), the young Caccini was encouraged from an early age to participate in the musical entertainment at the Medici court, where she spent most of her life. Such a combination of favorable circumstances, in addition to the innate talent of this young woman, produced impressive results. Over a period of about twenty years, Francesca Caccini composed and performed numerous secular songs, madrigals, canzonettas, and dramatic entertainment for the Florentine court, where, by 1623, she was reputed to be the highest paid of all court musicians.

Caccini's main contributions to early Baroque music are her two extant works: (1) *Il Primo Libro* (1618), which contains an extensive collection of early monodic solo song, and (2) the opera-balletto *La Liberazione di Ruggiero* (1625), which, if not the first published opera by a woman, is reputed to be the first Italian opera performed outside Italy, in Warsaw in 1682. Aside from these two substantial works, most of her compositions were never printed, and those few that were have all but disappeared.

To integrate Francesca Caccini into the musical tradition that she inherited seems, on the surface, an easy task: just assign her a place with her father's contemporaries in the Florentine Camerata, with Giulio Caccini himself, or with Jacopo Peri (1561–1633); or include her with the Venetian composers Claudio Monteverdi (1567–1643) and Francesco Cavalli (1602–1676); or put her with the Roman composers Stefano Landi (1590–1655) and Luigi Rossi (1597–1653). This would be chronologically and culturally correct, considering that early Baroque music was dominated by Italian ideas from the leading musical cities and courts of Florence, Venice, Naples, and Rome.

But, although the first musical example presented here, an excerpt from her opera, is representative of the Florentine style of the early Baroque, the second example, a canzonetta, suggests a heritage that may not even be Italian. The roots of this type of solo song can be traced back to the lute songs of John Dowland (1563–1626), perhaps, or to the Elizabethan ayres, or to the earlier French ballate, which were dance songs combining popular poetry and music.

But if one decides to integrate the music of Francesca Caccini into the Florentine school, a description of *Le Nuove Musiche* and of the musical splendor of the Medici court is necessary.

Whereas the basic ideal sound of the Renaissance had been polyphony of independent voices, the new sound ideal of the early Baroque, as expressed by the Florentine Camerata, emphasized one melody, alone, supported by a firm bass and held together with unobtrusive harmony. The text dominated the music, instead of the other way around. Since the declaration of the words was of prime importance, the melodic line was often lavishly embellished and there was much tone painting of the text, thus introducing the element of vocal virtuosity. The earliest surviving compositions in the Florentine monodic style are Giulio Caccini's collection of songs written in the 1590s and published in 1602 under the title *Le Nuove Musiche*. This is the style in which most of Francesca Caccini's songs are composed.

From then on, Italian composers turned out many monodies, either as solo songs, songs in dancelike rhythms, canzonettas, or solo madrigals. (These should not be confused with solo madrigals composed during the late 1500s, which were arrangements of polyphonic compositions and not genuine monodies.)

The courts of the major cities competed with one another in producing operas or entertainments that flaunted the new singer virtuosi. What one court had, the other tried to get. For instance, when Duke Alfonzo d'Este of Ferrara took his women singers on tour in 1581, Giulio Caccini demanded the same novelty for the Florentine court, which he got and directed in 1584. The occasion? Prince Vincenzo's marriage to Leonore de Medici!

The Florentine court certainly had the money to buy whatever entertainment it desired. The leading family in Italy from the 1440s until 1737, the Medicis controlled Florence with their unrivaled wealth and their love of the arts. Michelangelo and Raphael were among the great artists who were helped by their patronage. In fact, it was Michelangelo's grandnephew, the poet and writer Michelangelo Buonarroti, who was Francesca Caccini's chief collaborator. Many of his poems and verses were used as texts for her musical compositions.

The advantages of growing up in both a famous family, in which her mother was a singer and her father a composer, and a famous court have already been cited as contributing factors to Francesca Caccini's emergence as a significant early Baroque composer. But there is one other factor that decidedly influenced her career, and that is her reputation as a virtuoso singer. It was precisely the development and cultivation of the female professional singer, beginning with the Ferrara singers in 1580, that paved the way for talented women singers to have viable and well-paid musical careers. In fact, a court position as a singer was one of the few musical avenues open to women. Should a woman have been trained in the art of composing by her family, by private tutors, or by court musicians, or should she be inclined to write her own songs, there was a good chance that her works would get performed if she were a renowned singer. Furthermore, the rapid growth of music printing meant that women performers sometimes saw their music in print. Such was the case with Francesca Caccini's female predecessors, Maddalena Casulana (1540–1583), singer and madrigal composer, whose books of madrigals were published between 1566 and 1586, and singer-composer Tarquinia Molza (1542–1583) of the Ferrara court. Thus with the development of professional singing careers for women came the incentive for creating new musical works.

Musical Examples
1. La Liberazione di Ruggiero dall'isola d'Alcina
(selection from the opera)

Based on the libretto from Ariosto's *Orlando Furioso*, this opera concerns the liberation of Ruggiero from the island of the enchantress Alcina. This selection is typical of early Baroque performance practice in its emphasis on the words, the musical accompaniment being of secondary importance. The solo voice is accompanied by harpsichord and cello, forming the customary basso continuo harmonic background, but short instrumental interludes occur between the verses.

The harpsichord begins with a simple broken chord figure, introducing the solo voice which enunciates the words in typical recitative style. One interesting feature of the text setting occurs on the last word of each verse, where a type of hocket (hiccup) device repeats one syllable several times before coming to rest on the final cadence.

Each verse becomes a little more involved in its use of melodic melismas, extensions, and/or repeats of phrases. The last verse is set in a higher range, and the last two lines of text are repeated with more solo melisma and different harmonies in the chordal bass accompaniment.

The first performance of the opera, which Caccini also referred to as a balletto, was so lavishly staged that it even included Spanish riding horses!

Translation of the Text

Since the sky and sea today give destiny
To you high heroism equal to an empire,
May it please you to hear, likened to Ruggiero,
Abandoning his love for the wicked Alcina.

As the ardor of his wife for her husband,
Love, like a vile countenance spewed forth from the evil witch
This magnanimous virtue of royal love
Gave playful spectacle to the royal heart.

But, having been scorned and therefore repentant,
With her pity I soothe my breast
And so I bear witness to one who does not believe
That love is the only god of every beloved.

2. Chi desia di saper,' che cos' è amore
("To whoever desires to know what love is")

A canzonetta for voice and Spanish guitar, this piece comes from Caccini's *Il Primo Libro* of 1618. It is written in a vivacious rhythm, in homophonic style, with clear major-minor harmonies, and with distinct sections to fit the seven-line lyrical poetry. The poem of four verses thus dictates a strophic setting. Because of the emphasis on precise declaration of the text, the musical effect might appear to be one of syncopation or uneven rhythm. The change to a slower tempo, contrasting the shorter middle three lines of text, makes use of considerable word painting, especially on such words as *furore* ("fury"), *penare* ("to suffer") and *ire* ("rage").

These slower sections also offer the singer a chance to ornament the melodic line, but it should be noted that Francesca Caccini's music contained written-out ornamentation. The strong chordal bass line is provided by the Spanish guitar, which also supplies a short introduction and an occasional interlude between verses. Typical of the instrumental canzona form, the guitar begins with fast, repeated notes preparing the way for the quick, jerky rhythm of the first two lines of the text. The poem, incidentally, does not have a consistent refrain; only the first and last lines of each verse are the same. However, Caccini's skilled handling of strophic form gives the effect of the first and last lines of each verse being similar to the expected canzonetta refrain.

To whoever desires to know what love is
I will say it is nothing but burning,
That it is nothing but pain,
That it is nothing but fear,
That it is nothing but fury!
I will say it is nothing but burning,
To whoever desires to know what love is.

To whoever asks if I feel love
I will declare that my burning is over,
That I no longer suffer torment,
That I no longer tremble, nor fear,
That I no longer enjoy every moment.
I will declare that my burning is over,
To whoever asks if I feel love.

To whoever counsels me to love
I will say I no longer want to sigh,
Nor to tremble, nor to hope,
Nor to blaze, nor to freeze,
Nor to languish, nor to suffer.
I will say I no longer want to sigh,
To whoever counsels me to love.

To whoever believes that love brings joy
I will say that the sweeter love is, run faster,
Do not give in to its desire,
Nor tempt its disdain and rage,
Nor test its martyrdom.
I will say that the sweeter love is, run faster,
To whoever believes that love brings joy.

Selected List of Works
Vocal

Il Primo Libro dello Musiche a una a due voci, a collection of short vocal
works for 1 or 2 voices (and continuo), published 1618:
    19 sacred solos
    13 secular solo songs
    4 duets for soprano and bass
Ariette e canzonette, a collection of arias and songs. Book of songs from

the opera-balletto *La Liberazione di Ruggiero* (modern reprint ed. by Doris Silbert, Northampton, MA, 1945)

Sacred

Il martirio di Sant'Agatta, a sacred drama (written with G. Gigliano)

Ballet

Il ballo delle Zingare (1614)
La Liberazione di Ruggiero dall'isola d'Alcina, ballet-opera (libretto from Ariosto's *Orlando Furioso*)
Rinaldo innamorato, ballet-opera (1616)

Theater

Festa della dame (M. Buonarroti)
La Fiera (M. Buonarroti)
La Stiave (M. Buonarroti)

Selected Discography

Dispiegate guancie amata (aria): Pathé PG 86
O che nuovo stupor Telefunken: AS 641088
O che nuovo stupor, for recorders: EMI 1 C187 05865/66
Songs: Leonarda #123

Selected Bibliography

Bowers, Jane. "The Emergence of Women Composers in Italy, 1566–1700." In *Women Making Music,* ed. Jane Bowers and Judith Tick. Chicago: University of Illinois Press, 1986.
Neuls-Bates, Carol. "Francesca Caccini: Singer Composer." In *Women in Music.* New York: Harper & Row, 1982.
The New Grove Dictionary of Music and Musicians, 1980 ed. S.v. "Caccini, Francesca," by Carolyn Raney.
Newcomb, Anthony. "Courtesans, Muses, or Musicians? Professional Women Musicians in Sixteenth-Century Italy." In *Women Making Music,* ed. Jane Bowers and Judith Tick. Chicago: University of Illinois Press, 1986.
Raney, Carolyn. "Francesca Caccini." In *Historical Anthology of Music by Women,* ed. James Briscoe. Bloomington, IN: Indiana University Press, 1987.
——. *Francesca Caccini, Musician to the Media, and Her "Primo Libro" (1618).* Ann Arbor, MI: University Microfilms, 1971.

Barbara Strozzi

(1619–1664)

The Venetian Musical Academies

Biographical Summary

1619	Born in Venice to Isabella Briega and the famous poet, librettist, and dramatist Giulio Strozzi (1583–1652), who were not married to each other. Giulio Strozzi officially adopted Barbara when she was nine years old.
1629–36 (approx.)	Studies with Francesco Cavalli, pupil of Monteverdi.
1635	Giulio Strozzi founds the "Academia degli Unisoni," thus establishing a base for his daughter's singing career.
1644	Publication of her first volume of madrigals (for 2 to 5 voices), on texts by her father.
1651	Publication of op. 2, *Cantate, arietta, e duetti*.
1652	Death of her father.
1654–64	All her publications dedicated to nobility or wealthy people, in attempt to secure more permanent patronage.
1664	Publication of op. 8. Dies in Venice.

Like Francesca Caccini, the virtuoso singer-composer Barbara Strozzi enjoyed all the benefits of growing up in a prominent musical and literary family, encouraged by her father, the poet, librettist, and dramatist Giulio Strozzi, to make a musical career for herself. But unlike Caccini's, Barbara Strozzi's musical career never reached court life or the public concert stage; it was confined to a very private sphere, the "Academia degli Unisoni," founded by her famous father, which met in the Strozzi home. And yet, Barbara Strozzi received substantial recognition during her lifetime, including the publication of over one hundred works, mostly arias and secular cantatas for solo voice and continuo, in the eight volumes she published between 1644 and 1664. Her output thus places her among the most prolific composers of secular vocal chamber music of the early Baroque.

During that period, Venice enjoyed the distinction of being the operatic capital of Italy, following the opening of the first public opera house there in 1634. The principal opera composers working in Venice included Claudio Monteverdi (1567–1643), whose *Ulysses' Homecoming* (1641) and *The Coronation of Poppea* (1642) produced a steady demand for new works. Monteverdi's pupil, Pier Francesco Cavalli (1602–1676), Barbara Strozzi's private tutor, composed forty-one operas, and Marc Antonio Cesti (1623–1669) wrote at least fourteen dramatic stage works.

But Venetian musical life was also centered on domestic musical academies, such as the "Academia degli Incognito," founded in 1630, whose membership boasted some of the poets, philosophers, historians, and writers of the day. When Giulio Strozzi, who had collaborated with Monteverdi and other established Venetian musicians, created the Academia degli Unisoni, he made his musical entertainments the showcase for his adopted daughter, Barbara. Thus she entered a private, privileged musical world in which she was the only woman.

Even though Barbara Strozzi was a well-known singer in Venice, famous for its opera productions, and even though she studied with one of the foremost opera composers, Pier Francesco Cavalli, she apparently never sang in opera. She certainly never wrote an opera. While her male contemporaries functioned in the public sphere, Strozzi never left her enclosed domestic one. Perhaps this accounts for the limited genres in which she composed: secular, vocal chamber music that could be performed for the elite in a seventeenth-century Venetian drawing room.

How to integrate her, then, into the musical life in Venice of 1637 to 1664 if her musical output cannot be compared to her teacher, Cavalli, or to his teacher, Monteverdi, whose main interests were opera? Since she was essentially a composer of secular cantatas, she would seem to belong more appropriately to the cantata tradition of the Roman composer Luigi Rossi (1597–1623) or her younger Venetian contemporary Marc Antonio Cesti.

To understand Barbara Strozzi's style of composition, one might review the nature of the seventeenth-century secular cantata. The word *cantata,* in its literal translation, means simply "a piece to be sung." In publications before 1620, it applied mostly to arias in the form of strophic variations. Later the secular cantata evolved into a series of several sections or movements, usually for solo voice and continuo, on a lyrical or dramatic text. The secular cantata, from the mid-1620s through the next fifty years, consisted, then, of arias, recitatives, duets, and choruses, based on a continuous narrative text that was either lyrical or dramatic. Some secular cantatas written around 1650 became known as "strophic bass cantatas," using the same bass line for different melodies.

In general, the secular cantata contained the same genre pieces, namely, arias, with or without refrains, ariettas, recitatives, and perhaps some orchestral ritornelli. However, the forms for these genres represented a fairly wide choice, dictated mostly by the text but combining elements of the madrigal, monody, dance song, dramatic recitative, and bel canto aria. For instance, Luigi Rossi became well known for his "free cantatas," yet he was one of the first composers to establish the form and subsequent standardization of the da capo aria.

Barbara Strozzi made free use of musical forms. Since many of her texts came from lyrical poetry instead of dramatic or narrative verse, she treated them in novel ways. In the style of *Le Nuove Musiche,* Strozzi made generous use of word painting in the setting of her texts. Also, she frequently wrote in the *stile concitato,* a style of heightened excitement, expressing some dramatic event or word in a quick tempo or even repeating the word or phrase several times.

Thus, Strozzi's musical style is intertwined with her choice of texts. Almost invariably, she chose lyrical poems about unrequited love, as though she were perennially singing the blues, although in a more lively style than one would associate with blues singing. The Strozzi scholar Ellen Rosand has suggested that Strozzi's preoccupation with this type of expression might be the result of the audience for which she was composing and singing. Debates in her father's Academia centered frequently on feminist issues of the heart, for instance, the "virtues of tears" or the "virtues of love." The following musical example is representative of her choice of lyrical text and her treatment of such texts.

Musical Example
Tradimento! ("*Betrayal!*") from op. 7, Diporti di Euterpe *on a poem by Giovanni Tani*

Tradimento, the word, or refrain, beginning and ending this arietta, means "betrayal." Composed in 1659, the form is free in its depiction of the text. There are changes of tempo and rhythm, sudden interpretations in the flow of the text, and frequent repetitions of single words. Sometimes declamatory but more often melismatic, "Tradimento!" is representative of a style that is clearly "singers' music." Strozzi included numerous performance indications in her scores: specific directions for tempo, dynamics, and ornamentation. This arietta is representative of the *stile concitato,* with its furious introduction framing the smaller sections, and returning at the end to "Tradimento!" almost in da capo style. Word painting is especially pictorial on the words *legarmi* ("to bind me") and *incaterarmi* ("that imprison me"). As in the recorded selection, Strozzi probably accompanied herself on the lute.

Translation of the Text
Betrayal!
Love and Hope want to make me their prisoner
And my sickness is so advanced
That I realize I am happy
Just thinking of it.
Betrayal!

Hope, to bind me,
Entices me with great things.
The more I believe what she says
The tighter she ties the knots that imprison me.

To arms, my heart, to arms against the unfaithful one.
Take her and kill her, hurry!
Every moment is dangerous.
Betrayal!

Selected List of Works
Vocal

Il primo libro de madrigali, 2–5 voices. 25 madrigals on texts by Giulio Strozzi (1644)
Cantate, ariette e duetti, 1–2 voices, op. 2 (1650s)

Cantate, ariette e duetti, 1–3 voices, op. 3 (1650s)
Sacri musicali affetti, libro I, op. 5 (1655)
Ariette a voce sola, op. 6 (1657)
Diporti di Euterpe, Cantate e arietta a voce solo, op. 7 (1659)
Arie a voce sola, op. 8 (1664)

Excerpts from some of these works were published in 1656 in two collections by her teacher, Francesco Cavalli: *Diversi eccellentissi mi autori moderni* and *Sogetti eminenti nella musica.*

Selected Discography

Cantatas: Harmonia Mundi HM 1114
Non ti doler mio cor: Claves D 8206
Rissolvetevi Pensieri: Claves D 8206
Amor dormiglione: Echo; OM Pathé PG 86
Songs: Leonarda #123

Selected Bibliography

Bowers, Jane. "Women Composers in Italy, 1566–1700." In *Women Making Music,* ed. Jane Bowers and Judith Tick. Chicago: University of Illinois Press, 1986.
The New Grove Dictionary of Music and Musicians, 1980 ed. S.v. "Strozzi, Barbara," by Carolyn Raney.
Rosand, Ellen. "The Voice of Barbara Strozzi." In *Women Making Music,* ed. Jane Bowers and Judith Tick. Chicago: University of Illinois Press, 1986.

Isabella Leonarda

(1620–1704)

The Convent in Novara

Biographical Summary

1620	Born September 6 into a noble family of high government and church officials, in the Italian city of Novara.
1636	Enters Convent of Saint' Ursula of Novara.
1635–41	Studies with Gaspare Casati (1610–1641), Maestro di Cappella of Novara Cathedral.
1642	First compositions, 2 motets for 2 voices, appear in Casati's *Third Book of Sacred Concerts*.
1665–1700	Most prolific period of composition (see list of works).
1686	Becomes Mother Superior of convent.
1693	Becomes Madre Vicaria of convent.
1700	Publishes book of motets.
1704	Dies in Novara.

As a nun in the Ursuline convent in her native city of Novara, Isabella Leonarda composed mostly sacred vocal music. However, in 1693, at the age of seventy-three, she published a set of eleven trio sonatas, and in 1696 a sonata for solo violin and organ continuo, which place her among the first Italian women to compose in the new Baroque instru-

31

mental genres. For the most part, collections of her work include sacred motets for solo, one, two, or three voices, written for a cappella voices with optional instrumental parts, or *con istromenti,* as indicated in her later scores. Other sacred works for liturgical use include litanies, psalm settings, vespers, responses, and four masses. Only four of her motets are based on nonliturgical texts, in the vernacular Italian. Fortunately, all of Leonarda's works are preserved in the *Biblioteca del Liceo Musicales* of Bologna.

Unlike Caccini and Strozzi, Leonarda was never known as a performer. From the medieval through the Baroque periods, the convents provided the stimulus needed for musical creativity, and a beautiful voice was not a prerequisite. Like the nun Hildegard, Leonarda expressed intense religious devoutness in her compositions; most of her works are dedicated to the Virgin Mary, although a double dedication is sometimes made to a living person of the nobility.

To integrate Leonarda into the Baroque tradition of sacred vocal music requires a dual perspective. Leonarda's output should be viewed, first, in the context of the women composers who preceded her—namely, the nuns from convents in the major Italian musical centers—and, second, in the context of male composers who wrote in similar genres. Both traditions are relatively obscure in most music history books, especially that of the nun composers.

Parents of young girls in wealthy Italian families often chose a religious life for their daughters. Thus a large number of musically well educated girls, some of whom composed music for their own liturgical use, populated the convents. In 1593, from the convent of San Vito in Ferrara, Raffaela Aleotti's *Sacrea Cantiones,* for five, seven, eight, or ten voices, was published; in 1609, from the convent in Pavia, Caterina Assandra's *Collection of Motets* was published; in 1613, from a convent in Milan, Claudia Sessa's *Two Sacred Monodies* were published; and, also from Milan, four books of sacred music, including motets, a mass, and eight-voiced psalms, were published between 1640 and 1650 by the nun Chiara Cozzolani. Leonarda thus inherited an established tradition of nuns who composed vocal music.

The tradition she inherited from male composers of sacred music was, as one would expect, more varied. In keeping with the performance practice of the beginning of the seventeenth century, sacred motets were written for one, two, three, four, or even more voices, with basso continuo accompaniment or with instrumental (mainly violin) accompaniment and/or interludes. But as the seventeenth century progressed, so did composers' renewed interest in polyphonic music. Thus, collections of mid-seventeenth-century Italian sacred music often contain both monodies and polyphonic settings of the texts.

The names of the instrumental composers of the mid-Baroque are well known—Arcangelo Corelli (1653–1713), M. Cazzati (1620–1677), Giovanni Vitali (1632–1692), and Giuseppe Torelli (1658–1709), among others, all of whom were writing instrumental concerti grossi, solo concerti, and trio sonatas. However, the names of Italian composers of sacred motets/masses are less familiar, with the exception of L. G. de Viadana (1556–1627), whose *Concerti Ecclesiastici* of 1602, 1607, and 1609 contained motets for two, three, or four voices with organ accompaniment. Viadana replaced the chorus with solo voices and used the organ to accompany them, thus representing a significant break with the earlier *stile antico*. Composers in the older style of liturgical sacred music, namely Giovanni Pierluigi da Palestrina (1525–1594) and his conservative follower Orazio Benevoli (1605–1672), preferred the a cappella polyphonic and/or polychoral style of church music.

But who were Leonarda's male predecessors, aside from Viadana, who broke away from the Roman tradition? They were mainly composers from northern Italy, who worked in relative obscurity: Alessandro Grandi (1575–1630), Janazio Donati (1575–1638), Tarquinio Merula (1594–1665), and Gaspare Casati (1610–1641), who reputedly taught Leonarda. Following the lead of Viadana, these men, during the first half of the seventeenth century, composed motets for smaller ensembles of one to four solo voices with basso continuo. Leonarda's contemporaries who published similar volumes of motets with and without instrumental parts and basso continuo include the following lesser-known composers: in Bologna, Cazzati; in Ferrara, Giovanni Bassani (1657–1716); in Padua, Francesco Petrobelli (d. 1695); and in Milan, Giovanni Brevi (1650–1725). Leonarda's sacred motets are, for the most part, written in the style of these contemporaries. Solo sections with chordal accompaniment alternate with polyphonic sections, also accompanied by basso continuo.

The tradition of composing an entire mass, of course, goes all the way back to Guillaume Machaut (ca. 1300), but the tradition of setting only three sections of the Ordinary of the Mass, namely the Kyrie, the Gloria, and the Credo, was a regional phenomenon of northern Italy in the seventeenth century.

Musical Example
Kyrie *from Mass op. 18*
1696

Leonarda's Kyrie is followed by a Gloria, Laudamus te, Qui tolis, Credo, Crucifixus, and Et Unam Sanctum, the whole mass lasting just over twenty-three minutes. All three masses from op. 18 are scored for four voices, two violins, and violin or organ continuo. In this example, the cello takes the lower part.

This three-sectional work alternates chorus, solos with basso continuo, and instrumental ritornelli. In contrasting solo and tutti, Leonarda alternates chordal and fugal textures. Changes of tempo and character are frequent, though mostly between the three main sections. The tonality is almost all major and minor, the Kyrie beginning and ending in A major tonality, but the Christe Eleison beginning on a half-cadence on E. The final Kyrie is a fine example of Leonarda's fugal writing, but the final Eleison is a well-formulated choral cadence—IV, V, I. The unexpected emphasis on the subdominant, in the final phrases, is not unlike the ''Amen'' formula of the German Protestant chorale. The instrumental ritornelli are in the style of Corelli, the chosen instruments being two violins and cello basso continuo.

The score of this Kyrie is published in *Historical Anthology of Music by Women,* James Briscoe, ed. Bloomington, IN: Indiana University Press, 1987.

Selected List of Works
Motets

Motetti à tre voci, libro primo (1665)
Motetti à voce sola, op. 6 (1676)
Motetti à uno, duo, tre, e quattro voce, op. 7 (1677)
Vespero à cappella della Beate Vergine, e Motetti Concertati, op. 8 (1678)
Motetti à quatro voci con le littanre della B.V., op. 10 (1684)
Motetti à voce sola, op. 11 (1684)
Motetti à voce sola, op. 12 (1686)
Motetti à una, due, e tre voci, op. 13 (1687)
Motetti à voce sola, op. 14 (1687)
Motetti à voce sola, op. 15 (1690)
Motetti à voce sola, op. 17 (1695)
Motetti à una, due, e tre voci, pure con istromenti, op. 18 (1696)
Motetti à voce sola, con istromenti, op. 20 (1700)

Masses

Messa, e salmi, concertati, a cappella con istromenti ad libitum, op. 4 (1674)
Messe à quattro voci concertate con istromenti, op. 18 (1696, published together with the motets, op.18)

Other Sacred Works

Sacri concerti à una, duo, tre, et quattro voci (1670)
Salmi concertati à 4 voci con istromenti, op. 19 (1698)

Instrumental

Sonata à 1, 2, 3, 4 istromenti, op. 16 (1693)

Selected Discography

First Mass, op. 18: Leonarda #115

Selected Bibliography

Bowers, Jane. "Women Composers in Italy, 1566–1700." In *Women Making Music,* ed. Jane Bowers and Judith Tick. Chicago: University of Illinois Press, 1986.

Carter, Stewart. *The Music of Isabella Leonarda.* Ann Arbor, MI: University Microfilms, 1981.

Jackson, Barbara Garvey. "Isabella Leonarda." In *Historical Anthology of Music by Women,* James Briscoe, ed. Bloomington, IN: Indiana University Press, 1987.

Elisabeth-Claude Jacquet de la Guerre

(1666–1729)

The Court of Louis XIV

Biographical Summary

1666 or 1667	Born into family of Claude Jacquet, instrument maker, organist, and harpsichordist.
1667–84	Louis XIV undertakes her education, which is supervised by his mistress, Madame de Montespan.
1677	July: French journal *Mercure Galant* refers to the child wonder who "sings at sight the most difficult music . . . accompanies . . . composes pieces and plays them in all keys. . . . For four years she has been appearing with these extraordinary qualities."
1678	December: The same journal calls her "the marvel of our century."
1683	French court moves to Versailles, but Elisabeth Jacquet remains in Paris.
1684	Marries organist Marin de la Guerre.
1685	Composes her first stage work, a pastoral, performed at the French court.
1687	Composes her first volume of harpsichord pieces.
1691	Composes her first ballet, *Les Jeux à l'honneur de la Victoire*.

1694	Writes and publishes her first opera, *Cephale et Procris*.
1704	Deaths of her husband and her only child, a son. Organizes a series of concerts at her home; also begins a series of public harpsichord recitals.
1707–8	Writes and publishes her first book of cantatas.
1717	Retires from public performance.
1729	Dies at age sixty-three, very wealthy and accorded critical and royal recognition, including a medal Louis XV had struck in her honor.

The composer of a ballet, an opera, three volumes of cantatas, numerous harpsichord pieces, and solo and trio sonatas, Elisabeth-Claude Jacquet de la Guerre enjoyed a distinguished career in both the private spheres—in court, under the royal patronage of Louis XIV, and, later, in her salons—and in the public sphere as a renowned harpsichordist and composer. Her many accomplishments must be viewed as unusual for a woman of her time, and the favorable circumstances in which she lived and worked must be noted.

Born into a family of harpsichord and organ builders, Elisabeth Jacquet came to the attention of the Sun King as a young child, when she stunned the French court with her improvising, sight reading, and performing on the harpsichord. Her musical education was, from then on, supervised by the king's mistress, Madame de Montespan, and then by the royal governess, later the queen, Madame de Maintenon. There is no historical record that as a child Jacquet studied harpsichord with any of the renowned harpsichordists of the time, such as Jacques Chambonnières (b. between 1601 and 1611; d. 1672), Jean-Henri d'Angelbert (1628–1691), or François Couperin (1668–1733), but it was not unusual for daughters of noble families to become pupils of these masters or for talented children to be brought to play before Louis XIV.

The court's musical and cultural activities under Louis XIV are legendary, particularly the ballets of Jean-Baptiste Lully (1632–1687), in which the king danced, and the theater productions by Molière (stage name of Jean-Baptiste Poquelin). Louis XIV ruled from 1643 to 1715, but after the court moved from Paris to Versailles in 1683, the nature of its musical entertainment took on a different character, not often associated with the Sun King. The king's tastes changed considerably after 1683, when the music composed for him reflected a new preference for religious or mythological cantatas and chamber music. Many trio sonatas and much solo harpsichord music were also composed for the Versailles monarch, including François Couperin's suites, the first of which were published in 1713, two years before the sovereign's death.

But the French court was not the only place where music was being composed and performed in Paris during the last half of the seventeenth century. Salons were held by wealthy women as early as 1653, and women were known to be among the performers, singing or playing the lute or harpsichord. One of the most famous patrons, independent of the French court, was Louise de Mollier (ca. 1615–1688), who was herself a composer.

Women associated with the court also acted as patrons: Lully's mistress, Marie Certain (d. 1711), was well known for the musicales over which she presided, and Louis XIV's cousin, the Duchesse de Guise, also conducted influential salons. Louis XIV's mother maintained her own private musical entourage, and Mesdames de Montespan and de Maintenon, who were responsible for la Guerre's education, organized their own chamber music concerts in Louis XIV's private apartments.

Thus the French tradition of women making music, although almost entirely as performers or patrons, was well established by the time Elisabeth Jacquet came before the attention of the king. The first generation of singers who had been trained by Lully could find opportunities to sing at the Académie Royale de la Musique, established in 1669 as the "Académie d'opéra" for women to learn singing. But for women instrumentalists, professional opportunities were dependent on impressing members of the court, which la Guerre did. She later established her own musical salons in her home, where her harpsichord performances attracted notable audiences from 1704 to 1717, when she officially retired from public performance. She lived to see the establishment of the public Concerts Spirituels (1725), which offered the public a forum for choral, vocal, orchestral, and chamber music works. As for the French court, five years after la Guerre's death a woman was appointed as the royal chamber harpsichordist, and she was none other than François Couperin's daughter.

Such was the musical atmosphere in Paris during la Guerre's lifetime. To place her in this musical-stylistic context requires a brief look at some of the genres in which she composed—pièces de clavecin (1687 and 1707), ballet (1691), opera (1694), and French cantatas (1707–15), reviewed in the musical examples section. Composing in all these genres, especially in the larger forms of ballet, opera, and cantata, was highly unusual for a woman of this time.

La Guerre's first book of harpsichord pieces, published in 1687 and unfortunately lost, was dedicated to Louis XIV. Since such a dedication required the king's consent, la Guerre's abilities were undoubtely held in high esteem.

Who were the other French harpsichordist-composers of her time? The long tradition that culminated in the suites of François Couperin, whose

Ordres were published between 1713 and 1730, included Jacques Chambonnières, teacher of both Louis Couperin (1626–1661) and Jean d'Angelbert, royal harpsichordist for Louis XIV from 1662 to 1674; Jean-Baptiste-Henri d'Angelbert, successor to his father as royal harpsichordist from 1674 to 1735; Louis-Nicolas Clerambault (1676–1749); Jean-François Dandrieu (1682–1738); Michel-Richard de la Lande (1657–1726); and Louis Marchand (1669–1732). The contents of la Guerre's harpsichord pieces of 1701 resemble a collection of two different suites. The following dances are included: two courantes, two sarabandes, three gigues, two rigaudons, a minuet, a rondeau, and a flammande with variations. Quite an assortment, pre- Couperin's *Ordres!*

In 1691, when la Guerre composed her first ballet, *Les Jeux à l'honneur de la Victoire,* to commemorate the French victory at Mons, she was following the tradition of the French court, as established by Jean-Baptiste Lully. Another famed ballet composer, Jean-Philippe Rameau (1683–1764), could not have influenced la Guerre in that genre, since he did not become known as a ballet composer until the 1730s.

The earliest extant work of la Guerre is the opera *Cephale et Procris,* composed in 1691, published in 1694, and first performed at the Académie Royale de Musique in Paris on March 15, 1694; it was subsequently performed in Strasbourg between 1695 and 1698, as arranged by her friend the priest, church composer, and conductor, Sebastian de Brossard (1654–1730), publisher of the *Dictionnaire de Musique* (Paris, 1703).

Under Louis XIV, a national French opera style had been established in 1670. Referred to as "tragédie lyrique" by Lully, it was based on a libretto of classical tragedy or Greek mythology, combining lavish ballet. *Cephale et Procris* followed this model. It was long (five acts) and was based on a Greek myth in which virtue wins out. La Guerre's ballet is scored for strings, flutes, oboes, bassoon, and trumpet; there are many choruses and twenty instrumental pieces, including interludes and dances. Musically, it consists of both rhythmic and free-flowing recitative, da capo arias, solo and choral pieces, and, in the style of the times, basso continuo, throughout. Dedicated to the king, the libretto was written by the poet Joseph-François Duché de Vancy (1668–1704).

The year 1707 proved prolific for la Guerre; she composed her first book of cantatas, her fourteen *Pièces de Clavecin,* her six violin sonatas, and her instrumental trio sonatas.

Musical Examples
1. *Instrumental Prelude from* Samson
2. *"Tempête" ("Tempest") from* Le Sommeil d'Ulisse
(The Sleep of Ulysses)

It is the genre of the French cantata that provides the following two musical examples. With the 1703 publication of *Cantatas françoises* by Jean-Baptiste Morin (1677–1745), the French cantata became established as a type of chamber entertainment, in which instrumental numbers, recitatives, and airs told dramatic biblical stories or heroic myths. Aside from la Guerre, who wrote her first cantatas just four years after Morin's publication, other composers of the new French genre included André Cazzora (1660–1744), Michel de Montclair (1666–1737), Jean-Joseph Mouret (1682–1738), and Philippe Courbois (ca. 1705–1730).

La Guerre's early cantatas are based on biblical stories, in keeping with the emphasis on sacred music at Versailles during the last decade of Louis XIV's rule. Her third book of cantatas, dedicated to the Elector of Bavaria, includes three extended cantatas, based on mythological subjects, which may have been intended for stage performance. Typical of the form, both *Samson* from Book 2 (1711) and *Le Sommeil d'Ulisse* (1715) contain a Prelude, resembling the French Overture in its slow, dotted rhythms, an "Air Furieux" or a "Tempest" number, and a Finale that provides "the moral of the story." These characteristic features alternate with the usual recitatives and airs. Both cantatas are scored for voices, strings, continuo, and a wind instrument, either flute or bassoon.

The Text of "Tempête" from Le Sommeil d'Ulisse
> Autour de notre Héros,
> Le redoutable Ulisse,
> Tout le ciel est rempli
> Des foudroyants éclairs.
> Il faut gronder les airs!
> L'univers allarmé craint nouveau naufrage,
> Tous les vents luttant contre les flots.
> Le vaisseau renversé,
> Cède à l'affreux orage, disparaît;
> Et la Mer engloutit son enfant.

Translation of the Text
> All around our heroic adventurer
> the mighty Ulysses,
> the sky is filled
> with flashing lightning.

The heavens are to blame!
The very universe fears another shipwreck.
All the winds battle the waters.
The ship capsizes and yields
to the hideous tempest; it vanishes,
and the Sea swallows up its child.

Selected List of Works
Stage

Pastorale (1685) (lost)
Cephale et Procris, an opera (Paris, 1694), 5 acts, tragédie lyrique

Vocal

Cantatas based on the scriptures:
    Cantates françoises, livre I, for 1 violin, basso continuo, and instruments ad lib (Paris, 1708)
    Cantates françoises, livre II, for 2 violins and basso continuo (Paris, 1711)
Cantatas based on mythical or other subjects:
    Cantates françoises, livre III (Paris, 1715)
La Musette, ou les bergers de Suresne (Paris, 1713)
Te Deum (1721)
D'airs sérieux et a'boire, songs (Paris, 1721–24)

Instrumental

Pièces de clavecin (Paris, 1684)
14 pièces de clavecin (Paris, 1707)
6 sonatas for violin and basso continuo (Paris, 1707)
2 sonatas for violin, viola da gamba, and basso continuo (1695)
4 trio sonatas for 2 violins, viola da gamba, continuo

Selected Discography

Harpsichord pieces: Oiseau-Lyre 75, 13, OL50183; Voix de son Maitre CVC 2118; Educo 4005; American Society AS 1006; Turnabout TV 34685; Musical Heritage Society 930
Cantatas: Leonarda #109
Cephale et Pocris, air (voice and orchestra): Oiseau-Lyre 50117

Selected Bibliography

Borroff, Edith. *An Introduction to Elisabeth-Claude Jacquet de la Guerre.* Brooklyn, NY: Institute for Medieval Music, 1966.

Erickson, Susan. "Elisabeth-Claude Jacquet de la Guerre." In *Historical Anthology of Music by Women,* James Briscoe, ed. Bloomington, IN: Indiana University Press, 1987.

Neuls-Bates, Carol. "Elisabeth-Claude Jacquet de la Guerre: Composer and Harpsichordist." In *Women in Music.* New York: Harper & Row, 1982.

The New Grove Dictionary of Music and Musicians, 1980 ed. S.V. "de la Guerre, Elisabeth-Claude Jacquet," by Edith Borroff.

Sadie, Julie Ann. "Musiciennes of the Ancien Régime." In *Women Making Music,* ed. Jane Bowers and Judith Tick. Chicago: University of Illinois Press, 1986.

PART TWO

The Classical Period

Anna Amalia, Princess of Prussia

(1723–1787)

The Court of Frederick the Great

Biographical Summary

1723	Born at the Berlin castle, November 9, youngest sister of Frederick the Great. She was to spend her entire life at the castle.
1740	Studies harpsichord and piano under Gottlieb Hayne, cathedral organist and court musician.
1753	Studies organ and violin.
1756	Writes the music for the king's birthday celebration.
1758	Studies counterpoint with Johann Philipp Kirnberger, whom she then employs as court composer.
1767	Composes marches for band.
1770s	Composes chamber music, mostly sonatas for three instruments, and a few vocal pieces.
1787	Dies after a long illness that robbed her of the use of her eyes and hands. Her music library is bequeathed to the Joachimstalschen Gymnasium in Berlin.

The daughter of Frederick I (1657–1713), King of Prussia from 1701 to 1713, and the sister of Frederick the Great (1712–1786), King of Prussia from 1740 to 1786, Anna Amalia, Princess of Prussia, enjoyed all the advantages of growing up in a rich cultural environment. The court of Frederick the Great, one of the famed enlightened despots of the second half of the eighteenth century, boasted a musical and literary entourage often compared to that of Louis XIV.

From all sources, including the composer herself, it seems reasonable to assume that Anna Amalia was an extremely gifted amateur composer, who began composing in earnest fairly late in her life, at the age of forty-four. What is particularly unusual is that when she finally did start to compose, she wrote marches for the military regiments of certain generals (reflecting her brother's political ambitions?), a genre that has rarely been adopted by women. Today she is more remembered for her music library collection, the "Amalien Bibliothek," which still exists in its entirety, than for her musical compositions. The collection contains autographed scores of Johann Sebastian Bach, among other eighteenth-century composers, and it is noteworthy that Johann Forkel (1749–1818), the German music historian, theorist, and first biographer of J. S. Bach, considered the Amalia collection the best of its kind. Willed to the Joachimstalschen Gymnasium in Berlin, it was transferred to the Royal Library in Berlin in 1914, and after World War I was divided between the Preussischer Kulturbesitz in West Berlin and the Deutsche Staatsbibliothek in East Berlin.

For the purposes of this study, the Amalia collection is important for revealing her high level of musical education, as well as her conservative musical taste. As likewise revealed in her own compositions, the Princess of Prussia exhibited a conservative style typical of the Berlin School at the court of Frederick the Great, and of the German *Empfindsamkeit* style of Karl Philipp Emanuel Bach (1714–1788).

The following composers were active at the Prussian court: Johann Philipp Kirnberger (1721–1783), whom the Princess employed in 1758 and with whom she studied composition; Johann Joachim Quantz (1697–1773); Karl Philipp Emanuel Bach; Friedrich Wilhelm Marpurg (1718–1795); and Carl Heinrich Graun (1703–1759). These men were not only able composers but also theorists and writers. In fact, the breadth of their musical knowledge and their writings, addressed to the rising middle class of amateur music makers and concertgoers, is particularly representative of the ideals of Enlightenment. The stylistic requirements established by the rationalistic school of thought demanded a simplicity that could be understood by amateur and professional alike, as is typical of Anna Amalia's music.

The Berlin School itself has often been referred to as conservative, with the exception of K. P. E. Bach's later keyboard works. The principal orientation of that group of composers was toward vocal works, such as those in *Odes with Melodies,* published in 1753, containing songs by J. J. Quantz and K. P. E. Bach, and toward extended theoretical discussions and writings.

The Princess of Prussia was undeniably influenced by her teacher, Kirnberger, whose conservative musical tastes are well documented, and perhaps by the earlier German composers Johann Philipp (1649–1725) and Johann Kaspar Ferdinand Fischer (1670–1746), who composed a fair amount of march music. Anna Amalia composed songs and a few other vocal works toward the end of her life, but, for the most part, she was known as a composer of instrumental music—after all, she was an accomplished harpsichordist and her brother was an accomplished flutist.

She was also an important patron of music. The soirées in her royal apartments were attended by artists, by such renowned writers as Voltaire, who was employed at the court, and by musicians from all over Germany. In spite of the fact that the Princess composed marches, sonatas, and vocal works, she herself was convinced that her importance lay more in what she did for others, as patron and court employer. This was not an atypical attitude of gifted women performers, not only of her own time but in the history of women in the arts in general.

Musical Example
March for the Regiment of Graf Lottum
1767

In the homophonic style of the Classical period, with its emphasis on melody supported by a chordal accompaniment in simple harmonic rhythm, this march exhibits Classicism's regular and symmetrical phrase groupings. However, rather than anticipating the classical march form based on the minuet and trio, the form of this march looks backward to the Baroque, to the binary form of the dance suite. Characteristic of Anna Amalia's conservative style, as learned from Kirnberger and as evidenced by her preference for the music of J. S. Bach, this march follows Baroque binary form rather closely:

$$\text{A} \,:\|: \text{B} \,:\|$$
$$\text{I--V} \,:\|: \text{V--vi--I} \,:\|$$

Similar march forms exist in J. S. Bach's *Klavierbüchlein für Anna Magdalena Bach* of 1725 and in the Suites of J. P. Krieger and J. K. F. Fisher.

Selected List of Works

4 marches for band (1767–78)
March for 3 trumpets, 2 oboes, and bassoon (1778)
3 sonatas:
    for piano trio in D major
    for flute, violin, and harpsichord in F major
    for flute, violin, and basso continuo
Serenata for chorus and orchestra (1774)
2 chorales (1778)
1 war song
1 vocal duet
Songs (1780)

Selected Discography

Regimentsmärsche (4):   Musical Heritage 660; Amadeo 6390

Selected Bibliography

Ambrose, Jane P. "Anna Amalia," in *Historical Anthology of Music by Women,*
    ed. James Briscoe. Bloomington, IN: Indiana University Press, 1987.
The New Grove Dictionary of Music and Musicians, 1980 ed. S.v. "Anna Amalia,
    Princess of Prussia," by Eugene Helm.

Anna Amalia, Duchess of Saxe-Weimar

(1739–1807)

The Court of Weimar

Biographical Summary

1739	Born in Wolfenbüttel, daughter of Duke Karl I of Brunswick and the Duchess Philippine Charlotte, who was the sister of Frederick the Great and Princess Anna Amalia, on October 24.
Childhood	Thorough music education at the court: studies with Friedrich G. Fleischer (1722–1806), organist and composer.
1756	Marries the eighteen-year-old Duke Ernst August Konstantin of Saxe-Weimar.
	Begins to study composition with Ernst Wilhelm Wolff (1735–92).
1758	Husband dies, leaving her with two infant sons.
1758–75	Regent of Saxe-Weimar.
1776	Head of "Court of the Muses," Weimar. Composes the Singspiel *Erwin und Elmire*. Performance of *Erwin und Elmire*, Weimar, May 24.
1788–90	Tours Italy, as arranged by Goethe.
1799	Writes an essay praising Italian singing.
1807	Dies in Weimar.

As the niece of Frederick the Great and the daughter of his sister, this second Anna Amalia grew up in the musical court of Brunswick. Like her aunt, for whom she was named, Anna Amalia, who became the Duchess of Saxe-Weimar at age eighteen, was a composer in her own right, having received a fine musical education in her childhood, but considered herself a highly trained amateur in composition. Her list of works suggests considerable accomplishments in various genres, particularly the new German opera genre of the *Singspiel.*

In order to find a place for her in traditional music history, one might first explore the nature of the court life at Weimar over which Anna Amalia presided from 1758 until her son took over in 1775, and, second, review the names of the German composers of Singspiel who were active at that time.

Shortly after her marriage to the Duke of Saxe-Weimar, Anna Amalia employed Ernst Wilhelm Wolff (1735–1792), the composer of twenty Singspiels, to give her private lessons in music composition and to teach her young sons the art of music. This was the beginning of her assembling a court at Weimar that would later be referred to as the *Musenhof*— the court of muses.

Perhaps better known for its aggregation of poets and writers, the court of muses included the leading literary names of the German Enlightenment: Christoph Martin Wieland (1733–1813), Johann Gottfried von Herder (1744–1803), and Johann Wolfgang von Goethe (1749–1832), all of whom supplied libretti or poetry for the songs of the new German opera. Composers who worked in Weimar included Ernst Wolff, employed as organist, Konzertmeister, and Kappellmeister, and Anton Schweitzer (1735–1787), whose Singspiel *Alceste,* based on a libretto by Wieland, was heralded as one of the first real German operas following its performance at Weimar in 1773. Other Singspiels followed in the Weimar collaboration between Schweitzer and Wieland, and in 1775 an essay by Wieland entitled "The Art of the German Singspiel" prompted national interest in making this genre the popular alternative to Italian opera.

Actually, the Leipzig composer Johann Adam Hiller (1728–1804) should be credited with composing the first German Singspiel. Dedicated to the Duchess of Saxe-Weimer, his *Die Jagd* was performed, in Leipzig, a decade earlier than Schweitzer's *Alceste.* Other lesser-known German composers of these light operas were J. F. Doles (1715–1797), Georg Benda (1721–1795), and Friedrich G. Fleischer (1722–1806), whose Singspiel *Das Orakel* of 1771 also predates that of Anton Schweitzer. Anna Amalia studied with Fleischer sometime before her marriage and her move to Weimar.

The German Singspiel, like its predecessor, the English ballad opera, was a dramatic work containing many songs and quasi-recitatives based on vernacular or popular themes, as well as spoken dialogue much like the later operetta. Often referred to as "comic opera," the Singspiel was a lighthearted form of theatrical entertainment. It played somewhat the same social role in Germany as did the *opéra comique* in France. However, the romantic character of many of the libretti made the Singspiel, despite its simplicity and mass appeal, one of the forerunners of nineteenth-century German Romantic opera.

Musical Example
Soprano arietta from Erwin und Elmire
1776

This Singspiel, based on a text by Goethe, is representative of the popular style in the folksong-like character of its arictta and in its employment of strophic, or verse, form, similar to the vernacular songs of the time. In addition to a short instrumental introduction, the string ensemble is also used to comment on the text and to supply short interludes between the verses.

The Text
 Ein Veilchen auf der Wiese stand,
 Gebückt in sich und unbekannt;
 Es war ein herziges Veilchen.
 Da kam eine junge Schäferin,
 Mit leichtem Schritt und munterm Sinn,
 Daher, daher
 Die Wiese her, und sang.

 Ach! denkt das Veilchen, wär' ich nur
 Die schönste Blume der Natur,
 Ach! nur ein kleines Weilchen!
 Bis mich das Liebchen abgepflückt,
 Und an dem Busen matt gedrückt!
 Ach nur, ach nur
 Ein Viertelstündchen lang!

 Ach! aber ach! das Mädchen kam
 Und nicht in Acht das Veilchen nahm,
 Ertrat das arme Veilchen.
 Es sank und starb and freut' sich noch:
 "Und sterb ich denn, so sterb ich doch

Durch sie, durch sie,
Zu ihren Füssen doch."

Translation of the Text

A violet stood in meadow's green
Bowed in itself, unknown, unseen;
It was a darling flower.
Then a young shepherdess came along,
With a sprightly step and cheerful song,
She came along
The meadow with a smile.

Ah, thinks the violet, would I were
Of nature's flowers the one most fair,
For but a quarter hour,
Till I'd be plucked by this sweet maid,
And to her bosom fondly laid!
Alas, alas
For just a little while!

Ah, but alas! the maiden fair
For the poor violet had no care,
But crushed the hapless flower.
It sank and died, yet filled with joy:
"If die I must, yet I may die
Through her, through her
And at her feet may lie."

Selected List of Works
Singspiels

Erwin und Elmire, based on a text by Goethe (1776)
Das Jahrmarktsfest zu Plunderweisen, based on a text by Goethe (1778)

Instrumental

Divertimento for pianoforte, clarinet, viola, and cello
Harpsichord sonatas

Vocal

Songs (some of which were attributed to her teacher, Ernst Wilhelm Wolff)

An oratorio (1758)

Sacred choruses for 4 voices and orchestra

Selected Discography

Auf dem Lande und in der Stadt: Deutsche Grammophon 2533149
Sie scheinen zu spielen: Deutsche Grammophon 2533149
Concert for Twelve Instruments and Cembalo: Turnabout TV 34754
Divertimento for Strings and Piano: Turnabout TV 34754

Selected Bibliography

The New Grove Dictionary of Music and Musicians, 1980 ed. S.v. "Anna Amalia (ii), Duchess of Saxe-Weimar," by Anna Amalie Abert.

Maria Theresia von Paradis

(1759–1824)

Vienna and Beyond

Biographical Summary

1759	Born in Vienna, May 15, daughter of the Imperial Secretary in the court of Empress Maria Theresa, godmother of the child.
1761	Becomes blind.
Childhood	Under the guidance of Empress Maria Theresa, studies piano with Leopold Kuzeluch (1747–1818) and singing with Vincenzo Righini (1756–1812).
1770	Sings the soprano part in Giovanni Battista Pergolesi's *Stabat Mater* before the Empress Maria Theresa, accompanying herself on the organ.
ca. 1775	Becomes acquainted with Mozart.
1775	Antonio Salieri dedicates an organ concerto to her. Performs in Vienna's concert halls, and privately among the city's aristocracy and bourgeoisie.
1783	Tours Paris and London with her mother and her librettist, Johann Riedlinger. Visits Mozart in Salzburg. Gives concerts in Frankfurt, Koblenz, and throughout Germany.

1784	14 public performances in Paris, March–November.
	Concerts in London, November.
1785	Mozart writes a piano concerto for her (K. 456 in B-flat).
1786	Concerts in Berlin, Prague, and Brussels. Returns to Vienna. Performances at Vienna's *Tonkünstler Verein.*
1786–1808	Performances in Vienna and more concert tours.
1808	After the death of her father, founds an institute for music education where she teaches singing and piano until her death in 1824.

Pianist, organist, singer, and composer, blind from the age of two, Maria Theresia von Paradis was a prolific composer. Named for the Austrian Empress and Monarch Maria Theresa, who ruled from 1740 to 1775 and who employed her father as court secretary, von Paradis received all the benefits of a fine musical education, supervised by her godmother, the Empress. As a virtuoso pianist she toured Europe, becoming renowned for her phenomenal musical memory (which included over sixty concerti) as well as her pianistic skill. Her tours of Europe and frequent concerts in Vienna continued well into her old age.

Piano concerts were becoming popular in the last decades of the eighteenth century, and, in this respect, the touring pianist anticipated the coming age of the great Romantic pianists. Naturally piano works are well represented in the list of compositions by von Paradis, but so are vocal works: cantatas, songs, two operas, one operetta, and one melodrama. Hers is an impressive output.

To place von Paradis in traditional music history seems, at first glance, easy enough. After all, she was well acquainted with Wolfgang Mozart (1756–1791) and she studied with Antonio Salieri (1750–1825). Her lifetime musical career spans those of the masters of Viennese classicism: Franz Joseph Haydn (1732–1809), Mozart, Ludwig van Beethoven (1770–1827), and Franz Peter Schubert (1797–1828).

Who, besides Salieri, were her teachers, and what, if any, influence might they have had on von Paradis? Her first teacher was Leopold Kozeluch (1747–1818), with whom she studied piano from an early age and who, himself, was the composer of many piano sonatas and piano chamber works. The Bolognese composer Vincenzo Righini (1757–1812), while in service to Joseph II, Maria Theresa's son and successor, taught her singing. Karl Friberth (1736–1816), Kapellmeister at various churches in Vienna and author of several theoretical treatises, taught her music theory. The German Abbé George Vogler (1749–1814), organist, theorist, and composer of sacred works and numerous Singspiels, taught her dramatic composition and theory. Salieri, court composer and conductor of Italian opera, also taught her singing and dramatic composition.

Von Paradis thus benefited from a thorough music education with renowned masters who taught her not only in her performance media, piano and singing, but also in the art of composing and music theory. Given her enormous talent, patronage from the Empress, and her exposure to the best and most varied music education, von Paradis was well equipped to venture into the larger instrumental genres of piano concerti and sonatas.

The scores for her two piano concerti, the piano trio, the sixteen piano sonatas, and the two piano fantasies have, to our misfortune, been lost, leaving only three extant piano works: the violin-piano sonata (1800); the *Sicilienne,* included here, originally written for violin and piano; and a piano toccata in A major. Ironically, more of the vocal works survive: two collections of songs (1786 and 1790), her two operas, *Ariadne auf Naxos* and *Rinaldo und Alcina* (1797), her Singspiel *Der Schulkandidat* (1792), and her melodrama *Ariadne und Bacchus* (1791).

As prolific and remarkable as she was, von Paradis was not the only woman composer of note during the Classical period. Equally remarkable was her contemporary, the Viennese harpsichordist, pianist, singer, and composer Marianne Martinez (1744–1812), who studied keyboard with Haydn, singing and counterpoint with Nicola Porpora, played four-hand sonatas with Mozart, and composed 31 piano sonatas, 12 concerti, 156 arias, a mass, oratorios, cantatas, and a symphony! In Germany, the singer and actress Corona Schröter (1751–1802), employed as a chamber musician at the Weimar court, studied singing with Johann Hiller and wrote over forty songs between 1786 and 1794. Like the Duchess of Weimar, Schröter was also a friend of Goethe, on whose libretto she composed a Singspiel, *Die Fischerin*. In Paris, the singer, pianist, harpist, and actress Julie Candeille (1767–1836) composed an opera, several Singspiels, and also some instrumental chamber music.

All of these women, like von Paradis, became known first as performers, and only later considered composing as a viable alternative, then seeking out the best teachers in the art of musical composition. Their freedom to tour as either keyboardists or singers and to perform before the new middle-class audiences both enhanced their playing careers and produced, in return, more demand for original music. The burgeoning middle class of keyboard and singing amateurs was suddenly eager for new, accessible repertoire.

Like her contemporary Marianne Martinez, in her later life von Paradis founded and headed a music school in Vienna, with the express purpose of improving music education for women.

It goes without saying that von Paradis's blindness is another factor that made her composing career so remarkable. Von Paradis composed with a wooden pegboard, which used different-shaped pegs for different note values; this system was devised for her by her librettist, Johann Riedlinger. The fact that her compositions were notated and performed indicates that she was highly valued not only as a touring virtuoso but also as a composer.

Music Example
Sicilienne

Originally written for violin and piano but arranged for viola and piano and for cello and piano, as recorded on the accompanying cassette, this piece is probably the most often performed of von Paradis's piano chamber works. Its popular appeal seems to rest on two factors: the use of the familiar dance form, the Sicilienne, which Baroque masters had popularized in their keyboard suites and in pastoral scenes in operas and cantatas; and the undeniably beautiful, lyrical melody, which is almost Schubertian in its simplicity.

This Sicilienne follows the usual Baroque dance form, employing $\frac{6}{8}$ meter and dotted rhythms throughout, a sparse harmonic bass (here, the piano accompaniment). Cast in binary form, the first section ends in the relative minor, preceded by the Neapolitan-sixth chord. The second section begins and ends in the original major tonality, but two deceptive cadences using diminished chords expand the second half, which concludes with a brief return to the beautiful melody of the opening.

The musical score to *Sicilienne* is published by B. Schott Söhne, and can be found in *Historical Anthology of Music by Women,* ed. James Briscoe (Bloomington, IN: Indiana University Press, 1987).

Selected List of Works
Piano

2 concerti for piano and orchestra (lost)
1 piano trio (Vienna, 1800) (lost)
1 sonata for piano and violin (1800)
Sicilienne for violin and piano
4 piano sonatas (Amsterdam, 1778) (lost)
6 piano sonatas op. 1 (Paris, 1791) (lost)
6 piano sonatas op. 2 (Paris, 1791) (lost)

Piano toccata in A
2 piano fantasies (1807–11) (lost)

Sacred

3 cantatas (1791–94)

Songs

12 Italian songs (London, 1790)
12 Lieder (Leipzig, 1786)

Opera

Adriadne auf Naxos (1797)
Rinaldo und Alcina (1797), comic opera

Singspiel

Der Schulkandidat (1792)

Melodrama

Ariadne und Bacchus (1791)

Selected Discography

Sicilienne:
>   Arrangement for cello and guitar: Supraphon CS 392; Columbia 36352; Gramophon EA 1991
>   Arrangement for piano: Turnabout TV 34685
>   Arrangement for violin and piano: Telefunken 1286 & 642014; Columbia DA 1191; Decca DXSE 7179

Selected Bibliography

Neuls-Bates, Carol. "Maria Theresia von Paradis: Pianist on Tour." In *Women in Music*. New York: Harper & Row, 1982.
The New Grove Dictionary of Music and Musicians, 1980 ed. S.v. "von Paradis, Maria Theresia," by Rudolph Angermüller.
Pendle, Karen. "Maria Theresia von Paradis." In *Historical Anthology of Music by Women*, ed. James Briscoe. Bloomington, IN: Indiana University Press, 1987.

PART THREE

The Romantic Period—Songs

Louise Reichardt

(1779–1826)

The Romantic Spirit

Biographical Summary

1779	Born in Berlin to the composer Johann Friedrich Reichardt (1752–1814), Kapellmeister at the court of Frederick the Great, and Juliane Benda (1752–1783), singer, pianist, and composer.
1783	Mother dies.
Childhood	Family moves to Giebichenstein, near Halle. Studies with her father.
1800	Four of her songs appear in an anthology with her father's songs.
1808–9	Begins teaching singing, to support family.
1809	Leaves home to live in Hamburg. Begins to study with Johann Friedrich Clasing (1779–1829).
1809–1820s	Teaches singing in Hamburg.
1817	Organizes and conducts several women's choruses for the concerts in Lübeck and Hamburg to commemorate the Reformation.
1818	Prepares singers for Hamburg's music festival where Handel's *Messiah* and the Mozart *Requiem* are given for audiences of 6,000.

1819–1820s	Establishes a *Gesangverein,* teaching and conducting Handel oratorios, and translating into German the Latin texts of Hasse and Graun. The performances, however, are conducted by her male colleagues in Hamburg, as it is considered inappropriate for a woman to conduct a large mixed chorus and orchestra.

As the daughter of the composer Johann Friedrich Reichardt, Louise Reichardt grew up in the musical surroundings her father enjoyed as Kapellmeister at the court of Frederick the Great. At the age of thirteen, when her family moved to a small rustic estate in Giebichenstein, near Halle, the young composer-to-be participated in her family's entertaining of the literary greats of the day, namely, Goethe, Ludwig Tieck (1773–1853), Novalis (Friedrich von Hardenberg, 1772–1801), Clemens Brentano (1778–1842), and Phillipp Ludwig Achim von Arnim (1781–1831), whose poetry she used in her collection of twelve songs (1819).

Unlike most of the women composers discussed in this book, Reichardt did not have a performing career before she became known as a composer of songs. Furthermore, after the year 1809 Reichardt struck out on her own, leaving the protection of her family and supporting herself as a teacher, a choral conductor, and a composer in the distant city of Hamburg. In this way she typifies the spirit of the Romantic period, not dependent on patrons or royalty but determined to express the ideals of the times in her own individual way. She wrote most of her Lieder (songs) during the time she lived in Hamburg, from 1809 to 1826. Since the musical life of that city was dominated by a bourgeois society, Reichardt's rather folksy style was particularly accessible to the public for whom she wrote.

To integrate her songs into traditional music history is to invite a comparison with the foremost composer of Lieder, Franz Schubert (1797–1828). There are some similarities, particularly in both Reichardt's and Schubert's gifts for melodic lyricism. Reichardt was, beyond any doubt, a composer of memorable melodies. However, the simplicity of her piano accompaniments and of her harmonic language indicate a composer who was concerned, above all, with fidelity to the text; nothing should detract from the words of her chosen poem or literary source.

Perhaps, then, it would be more appropriate to include Reichardt with an earlier group of Lieder composers, those active in Berlin, including her own father. In the court of Frederick the Great, Singspiel was a popular form of entertainment, relying on folk material for many of its songs; its influence on the young Reichardt must have been pronounced. Representative of the Berlin School were Christian Gottfried Krause

(1712–1776), Johann Schulz (1747–1800), whose *Lieder im Volkston* (1782) became a model for this type of composition, Johann Friedrich Reichardt (1752–1814), Johann André (1741–1799), Christoph Nicolai (1733–1811), and Carl Friedrich Zelter (1758–1832).

The literary sources used by Louise Reichardt do not differ much from those of her contemporaries. German poetry proclaimed the Romantic ideals of communion with nature, religious fervor, yearning for death, romantic love, folklore, and sentimentality. Her uncomplicated musical style, as far as melodic text setting is concerned, is characteristic of the Romantic period, but her limited harmonic vocabulary, her uncomplicated rhythms, and her uninvolved piano accompaniments are more typical of the folk music style.

The personal life of Louise Reichardt must have affected her choice of texts. She was engaged to a poet, Friedrich Eschen, who died suddenly before the wedding. A few years later she became engaged to Franz Gareis, a painter, who also died before the wedding. From then on, Reichardt dedicated herself to her students in Hamburg, and toward the end of her life she became intensely religious, composing two books of sacred songs. Although she never conducted the Hamburg chorus in public concerts, she had an undeniable influence on the musical life of that city, as teacher, composer, and conductor.

Musical Examples
1. Hier liegt ein Spielmann begraben
(*"Here Lies a Wandering Player Buried"*)
1806

Based on the folk poetry as collected by Ludwig Achim von Arnim and Clemens Brentano in *Des Knaben Wunderhorn* ("The Youth's Magic Horn"), this song is typical of Reichardt's strophic settings of simple folk songs. The verses are short—eight measures—followed by a four-measure refrain, then a nine-measure piano conclusion. The piano accompaniment is based purely on an alberti-bass of broken chords sustaining tonic pedal point throughout. The harmonies of the verse represent only I, IV, and V, including its vii$_6$ function, and the piano conclusion uses only tonic and dominant harmonies. The performance direction is *bäurisch, lustig,* or "peasant-like, happy."

The Text
    Guten Morgen Spielmann,
    Wo bleibst du so lang?
    Da drunten, da droben,

Da tanzten die Schwaben
Mit der kleinen Killekeia,
Mit der grossen Kum Kum.

Da kamen die Weiber
Mit Sichel und Scheiben,
Und wollten den Schwaben
Das Tanzen vertreiben,
Mit der kleinen Killekeia,
Mit der grossen Kum Kum.

Da laufen die Schwaben,
Und fallen in Graben,
Da sprechen die Schwaben:
Liegt ein Spielmann begraben,
Mit der kleinen Killekeia,
Mit der grossen Kum Kum.

Da laufen die Schwaben,
Die Weiber nachtraben,
Bis über die Grenzen,
Mit Sichel und Sensen:
Guten Morgen Spielleut'
Nun schneidet das Korn.

Translation of the Text
Good morning, wandering player,
What's taking you so long?
Above and below,
The Schwabians are dancing
With a little Killekeia,
With a big Kum Kum.

Then came the women
With sickle and shovels,
And wanted to drive away
The dancing Swabians,
With a little Killekeia,
And a big Kum Kum.

Then the Swabians run
And fall into ditches,
Where they speak:

A wandering player lies buried,
With a little Killekeia
With a big Kum Kum.

Then the Swabians flee,
The women chasing them
With sickle and scythes
Across the borders:
Good morning wandering players,
Now harvest the corn.

2. Betteley der Vögel
("*Begging of the Birds*")
1806

Also taken from Arnim's and Brentano's *Des Knaben Wunderhorn,* the three verses of this folk poem encompass thirteen measures, following a symmetrical pattern:

4 mm. piano introduction, imitating sounds of birds
4 mm. first phrase, ending on a half cadence on the dominant
4 mm. second phrase, beginning in the dominant as key center and modulating back to the tonic
5 mm. last phrase, using I and V of the tonic.

The performance directions are *leicht und fröhlich*—"light and happy."

The Text
Es ist kommen, es ist kommen
Der gewünschte
Frühlingsboth',
So uns alles Leid
benommen
Und die kalte Winters Noth,
Welcher gute Stunden bringet,
Und ein gutes Jahr bedinget.

Kommen ist die liebe Schwalbe
Und das schöne Vögelein,
Dessen Bauch ist weiss und falbe
Dessen Rücken schwarz und fein;

Schauet wie es rummer flieget,
Und sich bittend zu euch füget.

Wollet ihr nicht sein gebeten,
Und mit etwas Esselwaar,
Kommen hier heraus getreten,
Zu uns oder dieser Schaar?
Gebt ihr aus des Reichen Haus
Nicht ein wenig Wein heraus?

Translation of the Text
It is come, it is come,
The longed-for
messenger of Spring,
So suffering and the
cold winter's need
Are taken from us all,
Which brings good hours
And determines a good year.

The dear swallow is come
And the pretty little bird
Whose breast is white and soft,
Whose back, black and fine;
See how it flies about
And bends entreatingly to you.

Do you not want to heed his prayer
And come out here
To us, or to his flock,
With a little something to eat?
Will you not share a little wine
From this rich house?

The musical scores to these pieces are found in *Louise Reichardt: Songs,* comp. Nancy B. Reich (New York: Da Capo Press, 1981).

The Romantic Period—Songs

Selected List of Works
Songs

12 German songs, of Johann Friedrich and Louise Reichardt (1800)
12 German and Italian Romantic songs, dedicated to Anna Amalia, Duchess of Saxe-Weimar (Berlin, 1806)
12 songs on poems by Novalis, Brentano, and Arnim
6 songs, op. 4, on poem by Novalis (1819)
6 Romantic songs, op, 5, on poems by Tieck
6 German songs, op. 6, on poems by Uhland
6 German songs, op. 8
12 songs (1819)
Other songs not included in collections

Sacred Songs

2 sets of religious songs, the last one written in 1823

Selected Discography

Songs (9): Leonarda #112

Selected Bibliography

The New Grove Dictionary of Music and Musicians, 1980 ed. S.v. "Reichardt, Louise," by Nancy B. Reich.
Reich, Nancy B. Introduction to *Louise Reichardt: Songs.* Women Composer Series. New York: Da Capo Press, 1981.

Fanny Mendelssohn Hensel

(1805–1847)

Domestic Music Making

Biographical Summary

1805	Born in Hamburg, November 14, granddaughter of the renowned philosopher Moses Mendelssohn and daughter of Abraham and Lea Solomon Mendelssohn. Eldest of four children, including Felix, four years younger.
Childhood	Mother teaches her to play the piano.
1816	Family moves to Paris, where Felix and Fanny study with Mme. Marie Bigot.
1818	Performs J. S. Bach's entire *Well-Tempered Clavier*.
1819	Composes her first song, in honor of her father's birthday.
ca. 1820	Studies piano with Ludwig Berger (1777–1839) and composition with Carl Friedrich Zelter (1758–1832), director of the Berlin *Singakademie*.
1822	Mendelssohn family begins Sunday concerts at their home, which will be continued by Hensel until her death.
1825	A letter from Goethe to Felix Mendelssohn states, "Give my regards to your equally talented sister." Composes a vocal trio, unpublished.

1827	Two of her songs published in a collection with works by her brother (Berlin: Schlesinger).
1829	Marries Wilhelm Hensel, a painter.
1830	Birth of her only child, Sebastian.
	Publication of three of her songs in a collection of songs, op. 8, by Felix Mendelssohn (Berlin: Schlesinger).
1837	Publication of one of her songs in an album for voice and piano (Berlin: Schlesinger).
1838	Her only public appearance as piano virtuoso, playing her brother's *Piano Concerto in G Minor*, February 27.
1839–40	Travels with her husband and son throughout Italy.
1842	Her mother dies. Hensel takes over the tradition of Sunday morning concerts at her parents' home in Berlin.
1846	Encouraged by Berlin publishers, she submits her *Lieder* op. 1 and her piano pieces *Songs Without Words* op. 2 to Bote and Bock, who publish them that year.
1847	Composes her last song, "Bergelust," in May.
	Dies of a stroke on May 14 while conducting a rehearsal of her brother's *Walpurgisnacht* for a Sunday concert.

Although Fanny Hensel wrote over four hundred works in the genres current in her time, with the exception of opera, the majority of her compositions were never published. The reason for this neglect is well documented. In spite of the fact that Hensel received practically the same musical education as her brother Felix Mendelssohn, the lack of encouragement from both her father and brother regarding her career as a published composer convinced the dutiful daughter and sister not to submit her works to publishers for many years. It was her husband, the painter Wilhelm Hensel, who eventually persuaded his talented wife to seek out publishers, which she did in 1837 and again in 1846, the year before her death. In 1850, several of her compositions, op. 8–11, including her piano trio, were published by her family. Although her diaries and some of her compositions are privately owned, many of her compositions are presently in the Mendelssohn Archive in the Staatsbibliothek, Preussischer Kulturbesitz in Berlin.

Even though her father and brother discouraged her from publishing, on the grounds that her domestic responsibilities and her feminine temperament mitigated against such activities, her mother and first teacher, Lea Mendelssohn, along with Wilhelm Hensel, tried to convince Fanny Hensel to overcome her hesitation to publish. In fact, it was through her mother, the Mendelssohn children's first teacher, that Fanny inherited a musical tradition of major importance.

Unlike most of the women presented in this volume, Hensel inherited a musical tradition through the female side of the family. Her maternal aunt, Sara Levy (1763–1854), was a gifted harpsichordist and student of Wilhelm Friedrich Bach; she later became an admirer and patron of Karl Philipp Emanuel Bach. Her daughter, Lea Solomon (1777–1842), Hensel's mother, was a student of Johann Philipp Kirnberger (1721–1783), who had been a student of J. S. Bach from 1739 to 1741.

This musical lineage helps explain why both Hensel and her brother often composed in the older Baroque genres of cantata, oratorio, prelude and fugue, and chorales, in addition to the contemporary genres of romantic Lieder, songs without words, and character pieces for the piano. Both children were also steeped in the music of Mozart and Beethoven, as evidenced by their use of Classical genres. Hensel's chamber music, including her piano trio op. 11, tends to look backward in its adherence to classical form and melodic phrasing, while looking forward harmonically.

Hensel was a formidable pianist herself, with a preference for the repertoire of J. S. Bach, Beethoven, and her brother, Felix Mendelssohn. However, in spite of the rise of the touring virtuoso pianist in the Romantic period, Hensel, with few exceptions, confined her pianistic appearances to the weekly concerts held at her parents' Berlin home.

At the Mendelssohn home literary readings, scientific discussions, and both sacred and secular concerts regularly featured such renowned poets as Goethe, Heinrich Heine, and Joseph von Eichendorff, whose poetry Fanny Hensel set to music. Other guests in the home included the scientist Alexander von Humbolt, the philosopher Georg Wilhelm Friedrich Hegel, the actor Eduard Deurient, and the writer Jean Paul.

Musically, Hensel was trained by conservatives; she studied piano with Ludwig Berger (1777–1839) and composition with Carl Friedrich Zelter (1758–1832). Her year's sojourn in France, studying piano with the virtuoso Marie Bigot, who was admired by both Haydn and Mozart, helped her develop her own pianistic style which she employed in the accompaniments to her songs and in her piano solo and chamber works.

The majority of Hensel's compositions are written for voice or piano, as was typical of the women of the Romantic period, who were encouraged to write in the genres appropriate for domestic or salon music making. Even Hensel's choral works were intended for the Sunday musicales in her home.

To place Hensel in traditional music history invites comparison with her brother, whose training and literary-musical environment were similar. But Hensel, as a song composer, might be better placed in the Lieder tradition, which began with the late Berlin School of Reichardt and Zelter and culminated in the songs of Robert Schumann. Her choice of German Romantic poets and her setting of the texts is more similar to the Schumann style than to the simplistic style of her Berlin predecessors. Likewise, her more involved piano accompaniments and her harmonic language, sometimes in response to the text and sometimes as purely pianistic preludes, interludes, and conclusions to the songs, represent a composer who exemplifies the later German Lieder style of 1825 to 1850. Hensel's songs have greater harmonic and tonal variety, greater structural diversity, and less symmetrical phrasing than those of her predecessors, Louise Reichardt and the Berlin School.

In spite of the fact the Hensel wrote in the larger genres of cantatas, oratorios, trios, sonatas, and quartets, her entire output was meant to be performed within the domestic or salon atmosphere. There is no doubt that, given the encouragement, Hensel could have written symphonies, as her brother did. A gifted and lyrical composer, Hensel is remembered mainly as a composer of songs, piano pieces, and an ambitious piano trio.

Currently, there seems to be a revival of interest in her music and her composing career as distinct from her brother's. Perhaps the time is now ripe for the publication and performances of some of the works in the larger genres that have, for the most part, been ignored.

Musical Examples
1. Nachtwanderer
("Night Wanderer") op. 7, No. 1
Text by Joseph von Eichendorff (1788–1857)
from Six Songs, vol. II, op. 7
pub. 1848

Typical of the Romantic period's emphasis on nature and mystery, Hensel's text setting of von Eichendorff's poem evokes a dreamy atmosphere. The slow setting begins and ends in a major key, but modulates in the third line of poetry to the relative minor. Tone painting is in evidence throughout, particularly on the repetition of the word *grau* ("gray") occurring on a diminished chord. In her quasi-strophic text setting, Hensel employs considerable flexibility in phrase lengths.

The Text

Ich wandre durch die stille Nacht
Da schleicht der Mond so heimlich sacht
Oft aus der dunkeln Wolkenhülle.
Und hin und her im Thal,
Erwacht die Nachtigall.
Dann wieder alles grau und stille.

O wunderbarer Nachtgesang
Von fern im Land der Ströme Gang;
Leis Schauern in den dunkeln Bäumen,
Irrst die Gedanken mir,
Mein wirres Singen hier,
Ist wie ein Rufen nur aus Träumen.
Mein Singen ist ein Rufen,
Ein Rufen nur aus Träumen.

Translation of the Text

I wander through the peaceful night
The moon, gentle and mysterious, steals out
from behind a blanket of clouds.
And here and there in the valley
the nightingale awakes.
Then once again all is grey and still.

O magical nightsong
from the distant land of streams,
a gentle rustling in the darkened treetops.
Thoughts skim across my mind;
my confused singing here is
like a call from a dream.

2. Warum sind denn die Rosen so blass?
("Why are the roses so pale?")
Text by Heinrich Heine from Six Songs, *vol. I, op. 1*
ca. 1837, published 1846

Also emphasizing the Romantic poet's interest in nature and romantic love, this poem receives a varied, though still strophic, treatment by Hensel. The opening questions of the text are set in the minor mode and in a slow tempo. However, the middle, shorter lines of the poem are cast in a major key in a faster tempo. The repetition of the last line of the poem, "Why did you leave me?" emphasizes Hensel's sensitivity to the text, where the melodic repetition serves as a kind of tone painting.

The Text

Warum sind denn die Rosen so blass?
O sprich mein Lieb warum?
Warum sind denn im grünen Gras
Die blauen Veilchen so stumm?
Warum singt denn mit so kläglichem Laut,
Die Lerche in der Luft,
Warum steigt denn aus dem Balsamkraut
Verwelkter Blühen Duft?

Warum scheint denn die Sonn' auf die Au,
So kalt und verdriesslich herab?
Warum ist denn die Erde so grau,
Und öde wie ein Grab?
Warum bin ich selbst so krank und so trüb?
Mein liebes Liebchen sprich?
O sprich mein herzallerliebsten Lieb,
Warum verliessest du mich?

Translation of the Text

Why then are the roses so pale?
O speak, my love, why?
Why then are the blue violets
In the green grass so mute?
Why does the lark in the air
Sing with such lamenting sound,
Why does the wilted blossom's fragrance
Ascend from the balsam herb?

Why does the sun shine down,
So cold and unpleasant, upon the pasture?
Why is the earth so gray, And empty as a grave,
Why am I so ill and gloomy?
My dear love, speak?
O speak to my heart, dearest love,
Why did you leave me?

3. Morgenständchen *("Morning Serenade")*
On a text by Baron Joseph von Eichendorff composed between 1837 and 1841

With its incessant rhythmic accompaniment and its perpetual motion tempo, Hensel's setting of this text represents a quasi *aba* or ternary form. Again, tone painting reinforces the Romantic poet's fascination with nature ("breezes in the treetops" and "forest sounds and bird calls"). In the middle of the song, the octave doubling of the voice and piano provide a startling contrast to the otherwise harmonically involved piano accompaniment.

The Text
> In den Wipfeln frische Lüfte,
> Fern melod'scher Quellen Fall
> Durch die Einsamkeit der Klüfte,
> Waldeslaut und Vogelschall.
>
> Scheuer Träume Spielgenossen
> Steigen all beim Morgenschein,
> Auf des Weinlaubs schwanken Sprossen
> Dir zum Fenster aus und ein,
> Und wir nach noch halb in Träumen,
> Und wir thun in Klängen kund
> Was da draussen in den Bäumen
> Singt der weite Frühlingsgrund,
>
> Regt der Tag erst laut die Schwingen,
> Sind wir Alle wieder weit
> Aber tief im Herzen klingen,
> Lange nach noch Lust und Leid.

Translation of the Text
> Fresh breezes in the treetops,
> From afar, melodic springing falls,
> through the loneliness of the crevices,
> Forest sounds and bird calls ring.
>
> Playmates of shy dreams
> All rise by morning light,
> Twigs are swaying in and out
> At your window,
> And we draw near, yet half in dreams,

And we announce what sings
Outside in the trees
The vast reason of spring,

When the day first stirs its wings
noisily,
We are all once more up and away,
But long after, there still rings
In the heart yearning and sorrow.

Selected List of Works
Choral Works

4 cantatas (1829–31)

Oratorium nach Bildern auf der Bibel, for soprano, alto, tenor, bass, chorus,
and orchestra (1831)

Gartenlieder: 6 songs for soprano, alto, tenor, and bass, op. 3 (Bote and
Bock, 1847)

Einleitung zu lebenden Bilder for narrator, chorus, and piano (1841)

Nachtreigen: Es rauschen die Bäume, for 8-voice a cappella (1929) Archive

Zum Fest der heiligen Caecilia, for 4-voice mixed chorus and piano (1833)

Smaller Vocal Works

6 vocal trios (1835)
6 vocal trios (1825–41)

Songs

12 songs with piano accompaniment by Felix Mendelssohn, op. 8, No.
7, 10, and 12 by Fanny Mendelssohn (Berlin: Schlesinger, 1830)

1 song in *Album* for voice and piano (Berlin: Schlesinger, 1837)

1 song in *Rhein-Sagen und Lieder* (Köln und Bonn: J. M. Dunst, 1839)

6 songs for 1 voice and piano accompaniment, Vol. 1, op. 1 (Berlin:
Bote and Bock, 1846)

6 songs for voice and piano accompaniment, Vol. 2, op. 7 (Berlin: Bote
and Bock, 1848)

6 songs with piano accompaniment, op. 9 (Leipzig: Breitkopf and Härtel, 1850)

5 songs with piano accompaniment, op. 10 (Leipzig: Breitkopf and Härtel, 1850)

1 aria for soprano and piano (Mendelssohn Archive, 1831)

Orchestral Works

Overture in C Major, for orchestra (Mendelssohn, 1830)

Chamber Music

Trio, for piano, violin, and cello, op. 2 (Leipzig: Breitkopf and Härtel, 1850)
Adagio, for violin and piano (Archive, 1823)
Capriccio, for cello and piano in A major (1829)
Sonata, for cello and piano
Piano Quartet in A Major (Archive, 1823)
String Quartet in C Minor (Archive, 1834)

Organ Music

Prelude in F Major, for organ (1829)
Prelude in G Major, for organ

Piano Music

4 songs without words, Vol. 1, op. 2 (Berlin: Bote and Bock, 1846)
6 melodies for piano, Vol. 1, op. 4, Nos. 1–3
6 melodies for piano, Vol. 2, op. 5, Nos. 4–6 (Berlin: Schlesinger, 1847)
4 songs without words, for piano, Vol. 2, op. 6 (Berlin: Bote and Bock, 1847)
Pastorella for piano (Berlin: Bote and Bock, 1848)
2 bagatelles for students (Berlin: Trautwein, 1848)
4 songs without words, for piano, op. 8 (Leipzig: Breitkopf and Härtel, 1850)
12 character pieces for piano (Archive, 1841)
Prelude and fugue, largo, praeludium, toccata
Piano Sonata in C Minor (Archive, 1824)
Piano Sonata in G Major (Archive, 1843)

Selected Discography

Songs (6): Leonarda # 112
Melodies, piano: Musical Heritage 4163
Prelude in E Minor for piano: Turnabout TV 34685
Trio in D Minor, op. 11: Crystal Records A 642; Vox SVBX 5112

Oratorium nach Bildern auf der Bibel: Best=NR 999.009
Lieder and Organ Prelude: Northeastern NB 213

Selected Bibliography

Citron, Marcia. "Women and the Lied, 1775–1850." In *Women Making Music,*
ed. Jane Bowen and Judith Tick. Chicago: University of Illinois Press, 1986.
——— . "Fanny Mendelssohn Hensel." In *Historical Anthology of Music by Women.*
James Briscoe, ed. Bloomington, IN: Indiana University Press, 1987.
———, ed., comp., and trans. *The Letters of Fanny Hensel to Felix Mendelssohn.* New
York: Pendragon Press, 1986.
Neuls-Bates, Carol. "Fanny Mendelssohn Hensel." In *Women in Music.* New
York: Harper & Row, 1982.
The New Grove Dictionary of Music and Musicians, 1980 ed. S.V. "Hensel, Fanny
Mendelssohn," by Karl Heinz Koehler.
Sirota, Victoria. "Fanny Hensel." Introduction to *Trio in D Minor,* op. 11.
New York: Da Capo Press, 1980.

Josephine Lang
(1815–1880)
The Public Sphere

Biographical Summary

1815	Born into the musical court at Munich, March 14, where her mother is an opera singer and her father a court musician.
Childhood	Her mother and a Fräulein Berlinghof teach her piano and singing.
1830	In Berlin, meets Felix Mendelssohn, who highly praises her singing and composing gifts.
1834	Meets pianist Stephen Heller on a trip to Augsburg.
1836	Becomes a professional singer at the Munich court.
1837	Schumann reviews her song "Das Traumbild" (op. 28, No. 1) in his *Neue Zeitschrift für Musik.*
1837–43	Her most productive period as composer. Almost one-third of her published works date from these six years.
1842	Marries Christian Reinhold Koestlin, amateur poet and professor of law at Tübingen University. Moves to Tübingen.
1842–56	Her home becomes a meeting place for southern German poets.

1843–56	Births of six children. Composing career comes to a halt; only four new songs written between 1844 and 1856.
1856	Death of her husband. Begins teaching career (voice and piano) to support her six children.
1859	Resumes composing career, asking her friend Ferdinand Hiller (1811–1885) to help publish her songs.
1862	Hiller helps Lang publish her op. 38, a set of six songs, dedicated to him. Composes first piano works.
1868	Hiller includes Lang's op. 12 and op. 14 in his book *Aus dem Tonleben unserer Zeit* (Leipzig, 1868).
1868–80	Public recognition of her work.
1880	Dies in Tübingen.

The composer of over 150 songs and numerous solo piano pieces, Josephine Lang was one of the most published women composers of the Romantic period. Most of her songs were published during her lifetime, and two years after her death Breitkopf and Härtel issued a two-volume set of her songs. Furthermore, many reviews of her songs appeared in the press during her lifetime, particularly in Robert Schumann's *Die Neue Zeitschrift für Musik* ("The New Journal for Music") as well as in the *Allgemeine Musikalische Zeitung* ("General Music Newspaper"). Many reviews praised her work, and she was considered a rather progressive composer of Lieder. Trained as both a singer and a pianist, Lang's piano pieces included mazurkas, character pieces, and songs without words, among others.

In contrast to Fanny Hensel, Josephine Lang enjoyed the encouragement of the major composers of the time: Felix Mendelssohn (1809–1847), Robert Schumann (1810–1856), the pianist Stephen Heller (1813–1888), Clara Schumann (1819–1896), Ferdinand Hiller (1811–1885), and a lesser-known composer of Lieder, Robert Franz (1815–1892). As early as 1830, the young Felix Mendelssohn was so impressed by Lang that he visited her every day for several months in 1830 and 1831, giving her free lessons in fugue, counterpoint, and other theoretical subjects, encouraging her far more than he did his own sister. It is particularly ironic that Lang and Fanny Mendelssohn Hensel composed most of their Lieder during the same decades, the 1830s and 1840s, and yet it was Lang, not Hensel, who got attention from the press and the publishers.

Although biographical sources confirm Lang's important associations with the major composers of the day, not much is mentioned of her association with the literary greats. She made abundant use of the poetry of Heine, Goethe, and Johann von Schiller, and she also set the poems of Ludwig Uhland and Lord George Gordon Byron. And a large number of songs were written on texts by Christian Reinhold Koestlin, an amateur poet, a lawyer by profession, and her future husband. Their two-year love affair, between 1840 and 1842, resulted in Lang's composing over forty Lieder based on his texts, most of which were written in the summer of 1840.

What is known about her own literary sensibilities is that after 1840 she frequently chose texts that held an autobiographical significance for her. Following the example of Robert Schumann, whom she came to admire tremendously, she was attracted to the literary-musical expression of something in her own personality or in her own life experience.

To understand how her later choice of texts may have reflected autobiographical feelings, it is important to explore some of the upheavals in her personal life. First, there was the separation from her lover, who, after becoming engaged to Lang in the summer of 1840, disappeared overnight, explaining to her in a letter that he had gone off to see his former beloved. Lang never answered his letter, and lived the following year feeling hopelessly dejected and lonely. When Koestlin returned the next year, they became engaged again and married in 1842.

From then on, physical and mental illness plagued her family: her second son became a helpless cripple; her husband died tragically in 1856; her eldest son, at age twenty-three, became paranoid and was sent to an asylum where he perished in a fire; her third son, Eugene, suffered from a nervous fever and, unable to work, lived at home. When her crippled son, Theobold, died in 1873, Lang began to compose sacred songs. After Eugene died in 1880, leaving her with only one of her four sons, Lang again took refuge in composing. In December of the same year she died of a heart attack. Of her six children, two continued the Lang musical legacy: Heinrich (1846–1907) published a biography of his mother in Leipzig (1881), and Maria Fellinger (d. 1925), who became a close friend of Johannes Brahms in Vienna, introduced the famous composer to her mother's songs.

To place Josephine Lang, the composer of songs, into nineteenth-century music history, one might include her with Schubert (d. 1828), Mendelssohn (d. 1847), and Schumann (d. 1856). Indeed most of her songs composed in the 1830s and 1840s show a dual allegiance to the latter two composers. Lang followed Mendelssohn's formal ideals in setting mostly strophic or modified strophic songs, with the piano accompaniment adding richness and texture but not overshadowing the text. Through the influence of Schumann, her harmonic vocabulary expanded. When she resumed her composing career in the 1860s, she continued in the Mendelssohn-Schumann tradition, although the genre of the solo song had, by then, taken on new forms of expression in the Lieder of Johannes Brahms and Franz Liszt.

Musical Examples
1. Der Winter *("Winter") op. 15, No. 5*
On a text by C. Feldman
1834

The tempo marking is *Allegretto mosso*. Although there is no piano introduction, there is a four-measure interlude plus an *a tempo* piano conclusion of eight measures. Again, expressive markings are explicit, complete with rallentandos and fermatas. The melodic range is an octave plus a third, but the harmonic vocabulary remains relatively simple. Cast in a minor key, the only modulation is to the relative major.

The Text

Der Winter ist ein böser Gast,
Ich fürcht' ihn wie Gespenster,
Die schönste Aussicht raubt er mir
Durch seine Doppelfenster!
Was nützen mir die Blumen all'
Die er an's Fenster malt—
Wenn nicht der Blumen Königin
Dem Aug' entgegenstrahlt.

Der Winter ist ein schlimmer Mann,
Ich fürcht' ihn gleich dem Tode.
Der ganzen Welt macht er was weiss,
Das wurde längst zu Mode.
Was Nützen solche Weisheit mir,
Der es an Licht gebricht!
Seh' ich das strahlend Augenpaar
Am Doppelfenster nicht.

Translation of the Text

O, Winter is a wicked guest,
I fear him as a ghost.
He robs me of the loveliest sights
by double-glazing my window.
Of what use to me are all those flowers
he paints upon the pane,

if the queen of flowers cannot
shine before my eyes.

O, Winter is a nasty man.
I fear him as I fear death;
he's forever making sport of the world;
'Tis always like that.
But of what use is such wisdom to me
who have discovered his tricks,
Since I cannot see that radiant pair of eyes
through this double-glazed window.

2. Frühzeitiger Frühling *op. 1, No. 2*
("The first sign of spring")
On a text by Goethe

Composed around 1830, when Lang was only fifteen years old, this
song is more involved than the preceding and the following examples.
Cast in the unusual key of B major, Lang captures the excitement of
Goethe's text, especially in the perpetual motion triplet accompaniment.
The rhythmic drive never lets up throughout the ten-measure strophic
setting of the text, the piano introduction, interlude, and conclusion.
There is considerable chromaticism in both the accompaniment and in
the vocal lines, whose range encompasses a tenth. Marked *Allegro agitato*,
this song employs subtle countermelodies in its unrelenting piano accompaniment.

The Text

Tage der Wonne, kommt ihr so bald?
Schenkt mir die Sonne, Hügel und Wald?
Reichlicher fliessen Bächlein zumal,
Sind es die Wiesen? is es das Thal?

Unter des Grünen blühender Kraft
Naschen die Bienlein summend von Saft.
Buntes Gefieder rauschet im Hain,
Himmlische Lieder schallen darein!

Leise Bewegung bebt in der Luft,
Reizende Regung, schläfernder Duft.
Saget seit gestern wie mir geschah
Liebliche Schwestern, Liebchen ist da!

Delightful days, are you here so soon?
Do you bring me the sun, hillock, and woods?
Is the rush of the overflowing brook
summoned by the meadows or the dale?

'Neath the blossoming vigor of Spring
buzzing bumblebees sup upon nectar.
Brightly colored feathers flap in the thicket,
from whence resound heav'nly refrains.

A gentle rustling stirs in the breeze,
a charming movement, an intoxicating fragrance.
Tell me, dear sisters, how it happened
since yesterday, that my beloved has come!

3. Wie glänzt so hell dein Auge
("How brightly your eyes shine!")
On a text by Agnes von Calatin

With a tempo marking of *Larghetto espressivo,* this love song makes frequent use of tone painting and mood setting through the following devices: alternation between major and minor, as found in the first two measures of the piano accompaniment, use of the descending minor seventh and diminished fifth, explicit dynamic markings, from *pp* to *ff,* and expressive directions such as *dolce, espressivo,* and *ritenuto.* The melodic range is wide, encompassing an octave plus a fifth. The harmonic vocabulary is rich, with implied augmented sixth chords but predictable modulations to the relative minor. The text setting itself is thirty-seven measures and is through-composed (not in verse form). However, the piano introduction, interlude, and conclusion remain the same throughout.

The Text

Wie glänzt so hell dein Auge,
So rein, so schön, so hehr!
Es ist ein klarer Himmel,
Es ist ein tiefes Meer!
Ach war ich doch die Perle
In diesem tiefen Meer!
Ach wenn ich doch ein Sternelein
An diesem Himmel wär!

Translation of the Text
  How brightly your eyes shine,
  so pure, so lovely!
  They are a clear firmament,
  they are a profound sea.
  Oh, if only I were a pearl
  in that deep sea,
  or if I were but the merest star
  in that heaven!

The musical scores to these three examples are found in *Josephine Lang: Selected Songs*, Women Composers Series (New York: Da Capo Press, 1982). The score to "Frühzeitiger Frühling" is also found in *Historical Anthology of Women Composers*, ed. James Briscoe (Bloomington, IN: Indiana University Press, 1987).

Selected List of Works
Songs

6 songs, op. 1 (1828)
Over 100 songs, op. 3–op. 28 (1830–43).
Miscellaneous song collections, op. 29–op. 45 (1862–71), sacred and
  secular
40 songs (1882; Breitkopf and Härtel)

Piano

Smaller genres of mazurkas, gavottes, character pieces, and songs without
  words, interspersed between op. 31 and op. 52.

Chamber

Herz, mein Herz, for cello and piano

Selected Discography

Songs (5): Leonarda #107
Lieder (9), for soprano and piano: Musica Bavarica MB 902

Selected Bibliography

Citron, Marcia. "Women and the Lied, 1775–1850." In *Women Making Music,* ed. Jane Bowers and Judith Tick. Chicago: University of Illinois Press, 1986.

——. "Josephine Lang." In *Historical Anthology of Music by Women,* ed. James Briscoe. Bloomington, IN: Indiana University Press, 1987.

The New Grove Dictionary of Music and Musicians, 1980 ed. S.v. "Lang, Josephine," by John Warrach.

Tick, Judith. Introduction to *Josephine Lang, Selected Songs.* New York: Da Capo Press, 1982.

Clara Wieck Schumann

(1819–1896)

Touring Artist and Composer

Biographical Summary

1819	Born September 13 to Friedrich Wieck (1785–1873), pedagogue, amateur pianist, and owner of a Leipzig piano firm, and Marianne Tomlitz (1797–1872), a gifted singer and performer in Leipzig. The eldest of four children.
1824	Mme. Wieck leaves her husband, seeking divorce. Clara Wieck assigned to the care of her father. By Saxon law, children are the property of their father.
1827	Formal piano instruction begins in June with her father, soon to be followed by daily lessons in theory, harmony, counterpoint, composition, singing, and violin.
1828	Friedrich Wieck remarries and the Wieck household becomes a center for publishers, writers, and musicians, for whom Clara always performs.
	First public appearance in the Leipzig *Gewandhaus*, October 20.
	Writes her first piano compositions, *4 Polonaises* op. 1.

1830	Robert Schumann (1810–1856) comes to live with the Wiecks.
	Gives her first complete recital.
1831–32	Makes her first extended concert tour, with her father, traveling throughout Germany and performing in Paris.
1831–34	Composes several piano pieces, op. 1–4 (Leipzig: Hofmeister). Performs extensively in Leipzig.
ca. 1835	Acclaimed throughout Europe as a gifted child prodigy; her admirers include Goethe, Mendelssohn, Chopin, Paganini, and Schumann.
1837	First tour of Vienna.
	Schumann formally asks Freiderich Wieck for permission to marry his daughter. A fierce battle ensues because Friedrich Wieck considered it an unsuitable match.
1838	After second Viennese tour, Clara Wieck is appointed "Kammer Virtuosin" to the Austrian court. The poet Franz Grillparzer honors her with a poem entitled "Clara Wieck and Beethoven." The press compares her to Liszt and Thalberg.
1836–39	Composes most of her piano works, through op. 11, published in Vienna (Haslinger; Diabelli; and Plechetti) and in Leipzig (Breitkopf and Härtel).
1840	Robert and Clara marry on September 12, after winning a bitter court battle to combat her father's refusal. Settle in Leipzig.
1840–43	Composition and publication of Lieder, included in her husband's op. 12.
1841	Birth of first child (of eight), Marie.
1842	Touring continues, as far north as Copenhagen.
1843	Birth of second child, Elise.
1844	Move to Dresden.
1851	Move to Düsseldorf, after the birth of six more children: Eugenie, Julie, Emil, Ludwig, Felix, and Ferdinand.
1853	Publication of many of her piano works completed (Leipzig; Breitkopf and Härtel).
	Johannes Brahms, age 20, first visits the Schumann household in September. He would become her lifetime friend and admirer.
1854	March: Robert Schumann's mental collapse and

92   *The Romantic Period—Songs*

	exile to the asylum at Endenich, where he remains until his death in 1856.
1854–64	Extensive concert tours, including Russia. Moves to Berlin, then to Baden-Baden.
1870s	Series of family tragedies, including death of two children and her father.
1879–93	Becomes principal piano teacher at the Hoch Conservatory in Frankfurt.
1891	Last public appearance, in Frankfurt, performing Brahms's *Variations on a Theme of Haydn*. Continues to teach at her home until her death on May 20, 1896.

One of the foremost pianists of her time, Clara Wieck Schumann enjoyed fame comparable to that of the leading piano virtuosi Franz Liszt (1811–1886), Sigmund Thalberg (1812–1871), and Anton Rubinstein (1829–1894). She premiered new works by Frederic Chopin, Robert Schumann, and Johannes Brahms, aside from programming several sonatas by Beethoven that had never been publicly performed. Furthermore, she was one of the first to play entire solo recitals. Her performing career was one of the longest sustained during the nineteenth century, lasting from 1828–1891 and including over 1,300 public recitals.

The life of Clara Schumann has been the subject of several biographies, the first of which was based on the reports and diaries of Schumann's eldest daughter, Marie, as recorded by Berthold Litzmann in 1902 and later translated by Grace Hadow in 1913 in *Clara Schumann: The Life of an Artist*. She is often mentioned in music history books, first as a pianist, second as the wife of Robert Schumann, and third as the object of Johannes Brahms's lifelong affection. Her musical reputation had remained that of pianist, wife, and devoted friend of Brahms until fairly recently, when attention was finally focused on the fact that Clara Schumann was also a composer.

Although music history and appreciation textbooks tend to ignore this fact, the recent scholarship of Nancy Reich and Pamela Susskind has made Clara Schumann the composer known to scholars of women in music. Many of her piano works have been reissued and recorded, but her songs have not fared so well. Perhaps her most well known composition is her Piano Trio op. 17 (1846), often compared unfavorably with her husband's piano chamber works. Naturally, considering her fame as a pianist, those who know of Clara Schumann the composer associate her primarily with piano compositions. But to mainstream Schumann's compositional output into music history, one must also consider her as a major contributor to the long line of composers of German Lieder.

Schumann's musical education, in the hands of her father, Friedrich Wieck, was thorough not only in the disciplines of piano, singing, theory, and counterpoint but also in systematic exposure to concert and operatic performances. Renowned as a musical pedagogue, Wieck saw in his daughter the ideally educated musician. Since she attended many operas and vocal concerts, Clara Schumann absorbed at an early age a style of writing for the voice. However, she became a Lieder composer only after her marriage to Robert Schumann, in 1840. Because the early years of her marriage provided new inspiration and new opportunities for exchange of literary and musical ideas, and because those early years witnessed the emergence of her song-writing gifts, it is tempting to consider Clara Schumann along with her husband in the history of German Lieder composers.

However, Clara's gifts were distinctly different from her husband's. Perhaps more in the earlier tradition of Schubert and Mendelssohn and not dissimilar to the songs of Hensel, Schumann's Lieder favor the subjects of the earlier German poets, namely, romantic love and the love of nature. Her musical settings display a delicate balance between words and music.

Although she was intimately acquainted with the great Lieder composer of the second half of the nineteenth century, Johannes Brahms, Clara Schumann's Lieder in no way look forward to that later style usually associated with Brahms, Hugo Wolf (1860–1903), Liszt, or even her husband's famous song cycles.

Clara Schumann herself did not feel that she was particularly gifted as a composer. She clearly saw her talents as inferior to those of her husband and her friend Brahms. Her admission that she could not take herself seriously as a composer leads one to examine the social climate for women composers in nineteenth-century Germany.

As in the case of Fanny Hensel, women composers at that time were rarely taken seriously unless they also happened to be star performers, in which case it was permissible to program one's own works in performance. However, reviews saying things like "considering the composer is a lady . . ." were not infrequent. Naturally the women composers could become insecure about the quality of their work.

Schumann considered herself first an interpreter, an artist; second, a mother; and third, a composer. Interestingly enough, Schumann rejected the belief that, as a woman, she should center her life around motherhood and domesticity. Her concertizing continued throughout her eight pregnancies, and when her own emotional and financial needs became greatest (during Robert's illness and death and her children's illnesses and three early deaths), Schumann found solace as well as income in performing and concertizing.

Although she had begun teaching piano as early as 1843 at the Leipzig Conservatory under Felix Mendelssohn, she did not devote herself to full-time teaching until the age of fifty-nine (1878). First and foremost, as her father had molded her, was her career as a concert artist, like her women contemporaries, pianists Marie Blahetka (1811–1887) and Marie Pleyel (1811–1875).

It is long past time for her compositions to be allowed to share the spotlight. It is unfortunate that Schumann herself compared her compositions unfavorably to those of her husband and other male composers whose piano music she performed. Now that more of her music is becoming available, Schumann is at last becoming recognized for her lyrical gifts expressed not only in songs but also in music for the piano.

Musical Examples
1. Das ist ein Tag der klingen mag
(*"This is a day for lively sounds"*)

This example comes from Schumann's last collection of songs, *Sechs Lieder aus Jucunde*, op. 23, by Hermann Rollett, composed in 1853 and published a year later by Breitkopf and Härtel.

Typical of the Romantic poetry of the first half of the century, the song glorifies and tries to imitate the sounds of nature. Schumann's setting is a lively one. It is through-composed, and integrates the piano accompaniment so thoroughly with the voice part that one can scarcely tell where one leaves off and the other begins. Likewise, tone painting occurs about equally between voice and accompaniment, especially in lines 5 and 10 of the poem. "Der Jäger bläst in's Horn" sounds, indeed, like a hunting call. And the concluding phrase, "Das ist ein Frühlingslied," provides a dramatic conclusion, with its crescendo and its melodic high note sounding on the most important word, *Frühlings* ("springtime").

The Text
    Das ist ein Tag, der klingen mag.
    Die Wachtel schlägt im Korn,
    Die Lerche jauchzt mit Jubelschlag
    Wohl überm hellen, grünen Hag,
    Der Jäger bläst in's Horn.
    Frau Nachtigall ruft süssen Schall,
    Durch's Laub ein Flüstern zieht;
    Das Echo tönt im Widerhall

Es klingt und singt all überall;
Das ist ein Frühlingslied.

Translation of the Text
This is a day for lively sounds;
The quail cries in the cornfield;
the lark exclaims with joyful call
over the bright green hedge.
The hunter blows his horn.
The nightingale gives a sweet call,
and cross the foliage a whisper travels;
an echo resounds;
chirping and singing everywhere:
It is the song of springtime!

The following three songs come from Schumann's earliest collection of published Lieder, *Zwölf Gedichte aus Rückert's Liebesfrühling*, originally published in Robert Schumann's song collection, op. 37. However, in the revised catalogue of Clara Schumann's works, these three songs are listed as her op. 12, published in 1841. The poet Friedrich Rückert (1788–1866), whose love lyrics in *Liebesfrühling* were published in 1823, was so popular among German-Austrian composers that he enjoyed the distinction of several early-twentieth-century composers' setting his texts to music. Among these were Gustav Mahler, Richard Strauss, Hans Pfitzner, Max Reger, and Alban Berg. Clara Schumann's settings, with the exception of "Er ist gekommen," composed earlier in 1836, are quietly simple, not dissimilar to earlier German Lieder composers.

2. Warum willst du And're fragen?
("*Why do you ask others?*")
op. 12, no. 11
1841

The piano introduction predicts the melody of the two verses. However, where the musical settings of lines 4 and 8, in the first verse, end on a half cadence, indicating the questioning nature of the poem, the piano finishes or answers the question with its harmonic resolution on the tonic key. When the questioning begins in the second verse, the piano then concludes its brief introduction on the dominant, and the voice answers, first in the tonic, then ending on an inconclusive subdominant, repeating the refrain of the second verse. The piano concludes the entire question-answer dialogue with a repeat of the introduction finally resolved in the original key.

The Text

Warum willst du and're Fragen,
Die's nicht meinem treu mit dir?
Glaube nicht als was dir sagen,
Diese beiden Augen hier!
Glaube nicht den fremden Leuten,
Glaube nicht dem elg'nen Wahn,
Nicht mein Thun auch sollst du deuten,
Sondern sieh' die Augen an!

Schweigt die Lippe deinen Fragen,
Oder zeugt sie gegen mich?
Was auch meine Lippen sagen:
Sieh' mein Aug', ich liebe dich!

Translation of the Text

Why do you want to seek advice from others
who do not share my faith in you?
Do not believe anything else than
what these two eyes tell you;
do not trust the word of strangers.
Do not heed your own delusion;
do not even interpret my actions;
but just look into my eyes!

Will your lips silence these questions,
or will they betray me?
Whatever else my lips may say,
look into my eyes, for I love you!

3. Er ist gekommen in Sturm und Regen
("He came in storm and rain") op. 12, no. 2
1836

This song is the most dramatic and exciting of this collection. One is reminded of Schubert's famous "Der Erlkönig," in the virtuoso piano part depicting "storm and rain" and in its restless through-composed form and driving rhythm. The piano's introduction and conclusion are the same, but even though the symmetry of the poem would suggest a strophic setting, Schumann's intent is to create excitement and drama, with minimal repetition.

Er ist gekommen in Sturm und Regen,
Ihm schlug bekommen mein Herz entgegen.
Wie könnt' ich ahnen dass seine Bahnen,
Sich einen sollten meinen Wegen.

Er ist gekommen in Sturm und Regen!
Nun ist gekommen des Frühlings Segen.
Der Freund zieht weiter, ich seh' es heiter
Denn er bleibt mein auf allen Wegen.

Translation of the Text

He came to me in storm and rain;
my anxious heart beat to meet his own.
How could I know that his destiny
would become one with mine?

He came to me in storm and rain.
Now the blessing of Springtime has come.
My beloved travels afar, but I watch cheerfully
for he is mine now, wherever he may be.

4. Liebst du um Schönheit
(*"If you love beauty"*) *op. 12, no. 4*
1841

In the slow tempo indicated, each verse of this strophic setting is comprised of two lines of poetic text, with the exception of the last verse which is characteristically extended with a repeat of the text. The piano part is unobtrusive, only commenting on the text which, again, is of a questioning nature: "If . . . then." There are no harmonic surprises, and the melodic range is moderate.

Both this song and the first were written during the Schumanns' first year of marriage. Her choice of Rückert's love poems is hardly surprising, and one is tempted to speculate that Clara's rather simple settings of the two slower songs echo her own belief that her gift of composing was minimal in comparison to that of her husband's.

The Text

Liebst du um Schönheit, o nicht mich liebe!
Liebe die Sonne, sie trägt ein gold'nes Haar!
Liebst du um Jugend, o nicht mich liebe.
Liebe den Frühling, der jung ist jedes Jahr!

Liebst du um Schätze, o nicht mich liebe!
Liebe die Meerfrau, sie hat viel Perlen klar.
Liebst du um Liebe, o ja mich liebe!
Liebe mich immer, dich lieb' ich immerdar!

Translation of the Text
If you are in love with beauty, then do not love me!
Give your love to the sun, with its golden tresses!
If you love youth, then do not love me.
Worship the springtime, which is young every year.
And if you love riches, do not love me.
Adore the mermaid who bears shining pearls.
But if you love for Love's sake, O then love me,
for I shall love you for evermore!

The musical score to "Liebst du um Schönheit" is found in *Historical Anthology of Women Composers,* ed. James Briscoe (Bloomington, IN: Indiana University Press, 1987).

Selected List of Works
Songs

3 songs on texts by F. Rückert, op. 12 (1841), originally published as Nos. 2, 4, 11 of Robert Schumann's *Gedichte aus Liebesfrühling,* op. 37
6 songs on texts by Heine, Geibel, and Rückert, op. 13 (1842–43)
6 songs on texts by H. Rollett, op. 23 (1853)
Approximately 10–12 solo songs on texts by Geibel, Heine, Serre, and Burns, composed between 1842 and 1846
Part-songs (1830)

Piano

4 polonaises, op. 1 (1828 or 1830)
Waltz caprices, op. 2 (1833)
Romance, op. 3 (1833)
Waltzes, op. 4 (1835)
4 character pieces, op. 5 (1836)
Soirée Musicales: toccatina, ballade, nocturne, polonaise, 2 mazurkas, op. 6 (1836)
Concert Variations, op. 8 (1837)
Impromptu, op. 9 (1837)
Scherzo, op. 10 (1838)

3 romances, op. 11 (1839)
Scherzo in C minor, op. 14 (1845)
Quatre pièces fugitives, op. 15 (1845)
3 preludes and fugues, op. 16 (1846)
Variations on a Theme of Robert Schumann, op. 20 (1854)
3 romances, op. 21 (1855)

Orchestral and Chamber

Piano Concerto in A Minor, op. 7 (1835–36)
Piano Trio in G Minor, op. 17 (1846)
Piano Concertino in F Minor (1847)
3 romances for violin and piano, op. 22 (1855)

Cadenzas

Beethoven Piano Concerto #3 (first movement)
Beethoven Piano Concerto #4 (first and third movements)
Mozart Piano Concerto in D Minor, K. 466 (first and third movements)

Selected Discography

Songs (7): Leonarda #107
Concerto in A Minor, op. 7 No. 1: Vox STGBY 649
Piano pieces: Vox STGBY 649; Candide CE 31038; Musical Heritage
    1339 and 4163; Pelican LP 2017; Orion ORS 75181/2; Harmonia
    Mundi 773/4; Bärenreiter BM 30 SL 1916; Nonesuch D 79007
Trio in G Minor for Violin, Cello, and Piano: Musical Heritage 1339; Phil-
    ips 688008; Decca DL 9555; Vox SVBX 5112; Decca UAT 273071
Variations on a Theme of Robert Schumann, op. 20, for piano: Orion ORS
    75182; Vox STGBY 649; Turnabout TV 34685
Lieder and Piano Pieces: Arion 38575
Variations, op. 3: Musicaphon BM30SL

Selected Bibliography

Litzmann, Berthold, ed. *Letters of Clara Schumann and Johannes Brahms, 1853–
    1896.* New York: Vienna House, 1973 (originally published in 1927).
Neuls-Bates, Carol. "Clara Schumann: Pianist." In *Women in Music.* New York:
    Harper & Row, 1982.

The New Grove Dictionary of Music and Musicians, 1980 ed. S.v. "Schumann, Clara," by Pamela Susskind.

Reich, Nancy. "Clara Schumann." In *Historical Anthology of Music by Women,* ed. James Briscoe. Bloomington, IN: Indiana University Press, 1987.

——. "Clara Schumann." In *Women Making Music,* ed. Jane Bowers and Judith Tick. Chicago: University of Illinois Press, 1986.

——. *Clara Schumann: The Artist and the Woman.* Ithaca, NY: Cornell University Press, 1985.

Susskind, Pamela. Introduction to *Clara Wieck Schumann: Selected Piano Music.* New York: Da Capo Press, 1979.

Pauline Viardot-Garcia

(1821–1910)

International Recognition

Biographical Summary

1821	Born into musical family in Paris on July 18, daughter of two opera singers, Manuel Garcia and Joaquina Garcia, and sister of singer and composer Maria Malibran and famous voice pedagogue, Manuel.
1824	Travels with her family to London, where her father is employed at the opera.
1825	Travels with her family to New York, where her father performs in the grand Italian opera tradition.
1826–27	Travels with her family to Mexico.
1827	Already fluent in four languages: Spanish, French, English, and Italian.
1828	Family returns to Europe; she accompanies her father's singing lessons on the piano.
1832	Death of her father.
	Begins to study harmony and counterpoint with Anton Reicha (1770–1836), even though Rossini wished to have her as a student.
1835–36	Participates in solo voice recitals and concerts with her famous sister, Maria Malibran.

1836–38	Studies piano with Franz Liszt, who encourages her to become a concert pianist.
1837	Gives her first public performance in Brussels, followed by other performances in Belgium and Germany.
1839	Makes her formal debut as an opera singer, in the role of Desdemona in Rossini's *Otello,* at the King's Theatre in London.
1839–40	Hired as prima donna for the Italian Opera season in Paris, by its director, Louis Viardot.
1840	Marries Viardot, twenty-one years her senior, and he resigns as opera director to help his wife advance her career. Temporary move to Italy, where she spends several days with Fanny Mendelssohn Hensel in Naples.
1843	Travels to Russia, where she sings not only the Italian repertoire in Italian but also the Russian repertoire in Russian.
1848–58	Extensive tours throughout Europe; also appears every season at the Italian Opera in London.
1849	Appears at the Paris Opera in Giacomo Meyerbeer's *Le Prophète,* which was written for her.
1859	On Berlioz's invitation, sings in his revival of Gluck's *Orpheus,* a role she performs 150 times.
1862	Retires from opera and moves to Baden-Baden, where she continues giving vocal recitals.
1871	Leaves Germany, because of the Franco-Prussian War, and reestablishes residence with her husband in Paris.
1871–75	Teaches singing at the Paris Conservatory, and later at her home.
1883	Death of her husband.
1910	Dies in Paris.

The most cosmopolitan of the women composers presented thus far, Pauline Viardot-Garcia lived in Paris, London, New York, and Mexico before the age of seven. At the height of her fame as a mezzo-soprano, she performed throughout Europe and in Russia, counting in her repertoire Italian, French, German, and Russian composers. Furthermore, she had an international set of musical and literary admirers: Schumann wrote his song cycle, op. 24, for her; Brahms wrote his Alto Rhapsody for her; Camille Saint-Saëns wrote his opera *Samson et Dalila* for her; Gabriel Fauré dedicated his songs opp. 4 and 7 to her; Gioachino Rossini wanted to have her as his student; and the Russian author Ivan Turgenev (1818–1883), who practically lived at the Viardot household, supplied her with librettos for her operettas, which she wrote for her family to perform. She knew almost every musician of distinction of her time, and she was friends with many writers, including Alfred de Musset and George Sand. She also had a famous sister, Maria Malibran (1808–1836), singer and composer, and brother, Manuel (1805–1906), the singing teacher.

Can one place such an international personality in the same sequence as her French contemporaries in the last half of the nineteenth century? True, she helped launch the careers and subsequent fame of Charles Gounod (1818–1893), Jules Massenet (1842–1912), and Camille Saint-Saëns (1835–1921). She was good friends with Hector Berlioz (1803–1869), and she was a champion of French grand opera, particularly of the composer Giacomo Meyerbeer (1791–1864). She admired and taught the songs of Gabriel Fauré (1845–1924). She also wrote one opera in the French grand opera tradition, as late as 1904.

But she lived for a while in Germany, and composed German Lieder between the years of 1843 and 1884. She also wrote many songs to Russian texts, which were translated into French or German for publication. To mainstream Viardot-Garcia into music history is to acknowledge that the second half of the nineteenth century, while often espousing nationalism in composition, witnessed an international sharing of styles and celebrities in Europe.

While Viardot-Garcia was primarily a song composer, of one-hundred-plus songs (sixty of which were published during her lifetime), she was also a composer of three operettas. Although they are unpublished, one, *Le dernier sorcier,* was performed in Weimar and Karlsruhe. Perhaps, then, she might be included with her countrymen Jacques Offenbach (1819–1880) and Charles Lecocq (1832–1918), whose operettas were performed all over Europe and whose styles were imitated by Franz von Suppé (1819–1895) in Vienna. And she wrote several arrangements for voice by such composers as Chopin, Schubert, Brahms, and Handel. Hardly just a "French composer"!

Toward the end of her life she became a much-sought-after teacher at the Paris Conservatory, her more distinguished pupils including the singers Désirée Artôt and Antoinette Sterling.

The Viardot home in Paris was a center for writers, musicians, and artists. From the happy marriage that lasted forty-three years, the Viardots had four children, all of whom were distinguished musicians. Louise Pauline Marie Heritte-Viardot (1841–1919) was, like her mother, a singer and a composer. The one son, Paul, was also a composer and a violinist, and the other two daughters became concert singers.

The following two musical examples illustrate Viardot's eclectic style.

The first follows the tradition of Robert Schumann, but the second is written more in the bravura style of French grand opera.

Musical Examples
1. Das Vöglein *("The Little Bird")*
on a text by Alexander Pushkin

The piano introduction, with its light melody and syncopated accompaniment, is a piece of tone painting in itself. Although the strophic treatment of the text is typical of earlier German Lieder, and the piano part suggests an integration between text and accompaniment typical of Robert Schumann, the concluding piano part, in parallel sixths, and the dramatic refrain forecast a new era in Lieder composition.

The Text
> Glücklich lebt vor Noth geborgen
> Gottes Vöglein in der Welt.
> Mühelos und ohne Sorgen
> Hat es leicht sein Nest bestellt,
> Schlummert leis im grünen Bäume,
> Gottes Morgenruf erklingt.
> Frühroth flammt as Himmelssaume:
> Vöglein schüttelt sich und singt.
>
> Nach des Frühlings kurzer Wonne
> Schwindet rasch des Sommers Pracht,
> Trüber Nebel deckt die Sonne,
> Schon ist nah des Winters Nacht.
> Wird's uns öder, wird's uns trüber,
> Fliegt zum Süden Vögelein,
> Über's blaue Meer hinüber,
> Fliegt zum neuen Frühling ein.

Translation of the Text
> Sheltered from danger dwells
> the happy bird in God's world.
> Without a care
> she has blithely built her nest,
> and sleeps blissfully in green branches as
> God's morning call sounds.
> With the first rosy flame, at the gate of Heaven
> the little bird shakes herself and sings!

After the all-too-brief delights of Spring
high summer swiftly passes;
a thick mist covers the sun,
and the Winter's night is already near.
Now everything seems duller and heavier to us;
but the little bird, winging her way southward,
high above the ocean blue,
flies towards a new spring.

2. Die Beschwörung *("Supplication")*
on a text by Alexander Pushkin

A dramatic setting of this Pushkin poem, "Die Beschwörung" dem-
onstrates a composer well versed in the French grand opera tradition and
in pianistic virtuosity. Both the difficult accompaniment and the chromatic voice part, complete with true operatic drama, cast Viardot-Garcia
into the later Romantic tradition of Franz Liszt (1811–1886) and perhaps
even Hugo Wolf (1860–1903).

The Text
    O wenn es wahr ist, dass zur Nacht,
    Die in den Schlaf lullt alles Leben
    Und nur des Mondlichts bleiche Pracht
    lasst um die Grabessteine weben;
    O wenn es wahr ist, dass dann leer
    Die Gräber stehn die Todten lassen,
    Erwart' ich dich, dich zu umfassen.
    Hör' Leila mich! Komm her! Komm heim!

    Erschein' aus deinem Schattenreich,
    Ganz wie du warst vor unserm Scheiden,
    Dem kalten Wintertage gleich,
    Das Angesicht entstellt von Leiden.
    O komm, ein ferner Stern,
    Daher, ein Hauch, ein leis Getöne,
    Oder in schreckenvoller Schöne,
    Mir ist es gleich, Komm her! Komm hiem!

    Ich riefe Leila darum nie
    Des Grabs Geheimniss zu erfahren,
    Auch nicht zum Vorwurf gegendie,
    Die meiner Liebe Mörder waren,

Auch darum nicht weil oft noch schwer
Mich Zweifel quälen.
Nein, zu sagen, dass treu, wie stets
Mein Herz geschlagen;
Es jetzt noch schlägt . . . Komm her, Komm heim!

Translation of the Text
    Ah, if 'tis true that night
lulls all life into a dream world,
and only the frail, wan moonlight
plays among the tombstones—
Ah, if 'tis truly at that hour
the graves yield up their dead—
'tis then I await your embrace.
Hear me, Leila, return home to me!

    Appear from your shadowy world,
just as you were before our final parting,
cold as a winter's day,
your face disfigured with pain.
O come back now, like some distant star,
come as a breath, a murmured sound,
or in some more frightening, beautiful guise,
no matter how, but come back home!

    I cry out for Leila, not
to learn the secrets of the grave,
nor to rail against those
who killed my love,
nor even because of the bitter despair
tormenting me now.
No, only to tell how my
shattered heart remains faithful;
it is breaking still . . . O come back again!

The musical score of "Beschwörung" is found in *Historical Anthology of Music by Women,* ed. James Briscoe (Bloomington, IN: Indiana University Press, 1987).

The Romantic Period—Songs

Selected List of Works
Songs

Over 100 songs, 60 of which were published by various firms: Breitkopf and
Härtel, Enoch, Schott, Schlesinger, Miran, Durand, and Bote and Bock.

Operettas

Conte de fées (1879)
Le Dernier sorcier, libretto by Turgenev (1869)
L'Ogre, libretto by Turgenev (1868)
Trop de Femmes, libretto by Turgenev (1867)

Opera

Cendrillon (1904)

Arrangements

6 mazurkas by Chopin, for voice (Breitkopf and Härtel)
Waltzes of Schubert, for voice (Schirmer)
Hungarian dances of Brahms, vocal duet (Hamelle)
Air de Xerxès by Handel, for voice, violin, cello, and piano

Piano

3 sets of pieces for 4 hands, including *Suite Armenienne* and a polonaise
3 albums of Russian melodies, 12 pieces each, including airs, gavottes,
and mazurkas

Selected Discography

Songs (3): Leonarda #107

Selected Bibliography

Caswell, Austin B. "Pauline Viardot-Garcia." In *Historical Anthology of Music by
Women,* ed. James Briscoe. Bloomington, IN: Indiana University Press, 1987.
Fitzlyon, April. *The Price of Genius: A Biography of Pauline Viardot.* London:
Calder, 1964.
The New Grove Dictionary of Music and Musicians, 1980 ed. S.v. "Viardot, Pau-
line," by April Fitzlyon.

Francesca Caccini

Elisabeth-Claude Jacquet de la Guerre

Josephine Lang

Clara Schumann

111

Pauline Viardot-Garcia

Louise Farrenc

Cécile Chaminade

Amy Beach

113

Rebecca Clarke

Katherine Hoover.
Photograph by Frank Giraldi.

114

Ellen Taaffe Zwilich

Ruth Schonthal

Barbara Kolb. Photograph by Jean-Luce Huré.

Marga Richter.
Photograph by Alan Skelly, courtesy of Magna Carta Management.

Judith Lang Zaimont

PART FOUR

The Romantic Period and Early Twentieth Century— Instrumental Music

Louise
Dumont Farrenc

(1804–1875)

Pianist, Composer, Scholar

Biographical Summary

1804	Born in Paris into a family of royal artists and painters, May 31; sister of the laureate sculptor Auguste Dumont.
1810	Begins piano studies, first with Ignaz Moscheles (1794–1859) and then with Johann Hummel (1778–1837).
1819	Enters the Paris Conservatory, already a proficient pianist, to study with Anton Reicha (1770–1836).
1821	Marries Aristide Farrenc, amateur musician, music publisher, and scholar.
1825	Finishes her studies at the Paris Conservatory, with interruptions for concert tours. Earliest piano compositions, 2 sets of variations.
1825–26	Founding of her husband's music publishing company.
1826	Birth of her daughter, composer and pianist Victorine Louise, her only child.
1825–39	Composes most of her piano works, published by her husband's firm, and later published in London and Bonn.

1842	Appointed Professor of Piano at the Paris Conservatory.
1841–47	Composes her 3 symphonies.
1844–55	Composes most of her chamber works.
1855–62	Composes more piano solo and chamber works.
1859	Death of her daughter.
1861 and 1869	Awarded *Prix Chartier* of the Institute of France.
1861	Begins work, with her husband, on *Le Trésor des pianistes*.
1865	Death of her husband.
1874	Completion of the 23-volume anthology, *Le Trésor des pianistes*.
1875	Dies in Paris.

Aside from being a prolific composer, Louise Farrenc made musical history for women because she was a scholar who published a twenty-three volume anthology of seventeenth- and eighteenth-century music; its introduction, on Baroque ornamentation, was published separately, in 1895. Furthermore, she was so revered as a piano teacher that she held the position of Professor of Piano at the Paris Conservatory for over thirty years (1842–72)—the only woman to have held a post as long at that prestigious conservatory. Among her more notable achievements as a composer are her works in the larger genres of symphonic overtures, symphonies, and piano trios and quintets.

To mainstream Farrenc into the French musical tradition of the early to mid- nineteenth century is not without its problems. Aside from the Paris concerts given by the famous pianists Chopin, Liszt, Sigismond Thalberg, and Henri Herz, the French musical scene was dominated by theater and salon music. The grand opera tradition of Giacomo Meyerbeer (1791–1864) and Charles Gounod (1818–1893) was running a close second in popularity, but the real flourishing of nineteenth-century Romantic French music was not to begin until the last half of the century. With the exception of the orchestral and opera composer Hector Berlioz (1803–1869), along with Gounod and Meyerbeer, French music was to experience a renaissance with the later composers César Franck (1822–1890), Georges Bizet (1838–1875), Camille Saint-Saëns (1835–1921), Louise Heritte-Viardot (1841–1919), Gabriel Fauré (1845–1924), Augusta Holmès (1847–1903), Henri Duparc (1848–1933), Ernest Chausson (1855–1899), Cécile Chaminade (1857–1944), and Paul Dukas (1865–1935).

The music of Farrenc, at times anticipating the later French Romantic tradition, still tends to be rooted in an earlier style. The forms and genres that she used belong to those of the Classical tradition, while her harmonic language and range of musical expression are more Romantic. Since, during her lifetime, Romantic piano music often emphasized salon pieces, Farrenc's masterful piano variations, chamber music, and symphonies can be considered something of an anachronism of the period.

Perhaps her style and choice of genres show the influence of her teacher, Anton Reicha (1770–1836), a prolific composer of symphonies, overtures, piano works, and chamber music. Farrenc studied with Reicha at the Paris Conservatory from 1819 to 1825.

Farrenc's compositional output can be divided into specific decades during which she composed in specific genres. Her earliest compositions for solo piano appeared between 1825 and 1839 and were issued by her husband's firm. These are mostly variations, rondos, or études. In 1836, Robert Schumann praised her "Air russe varié" op. 17 in his *Neue Zeitschrift für Musik,* and in 1840 the Paris music critic Maurice Bourges extolled her *Thirty Etudes in all Major and Minor Keys* op. 26 in his *Revue et gazette musicale.*

The decade of the 1840s witnessed the composition of her three symphonies and some of her earlier piano chamber music, and in the 1850s and early 1860s she produced a variety of solo piano music and more chamber music. The *Nonetto* op. 38 (1849), performed frequently during the 1850s, brought Farrenc such publicity that the director of the Paris Conservatory raised her salary to a level comparable to that received by male professors in the instrumental division.

However, Farrenc the composer was already well known. Berlioz had praised her orchestral skills as evidenced in her *Overture #2* op. 24 (ca. 1834). Furthermore, although her three symphonies had been performed in Paris, Brussels, Copenhagen, and Geneva, none was ever published.

In 1861 Farrenc became the first winner of the *Prix Chartier Académie des Beaux-Arts,* an award for chamber music composition. Later prize winners were to include Edouard Lalo, César Franck, and Gabriel Fauré, and Farrenc won the prize a second time, in 1869.

During the last fifteen years of her life, Farrenc became increasingly devoted to both teaching and music scholarship. One of her prize pupils was her daughter, Victorine, who won the *premier prix* for piano at the Conservatory in 1844 but whose death at the age of thirty-three cut short a performing career that held remarkable promise. During Louise Farrenc's thirty-year tenure as piano professor at the Conservatory, her thirty Etudes, op. 26 (1839), were adopted by the Conservatory as a requirement for all piano students. The études were reissued by Leduce Publishers ten years after her death.

A prolific composer whose music was widely performed and reviewed during her lifetime, Farrenc the composer, pedagogue, and scholar foreshadowed the type of success a few women would enjoy a century later.

Her immensely varied output, from solo piano music to overtures, symphonies, and a wealth of chamber music, merits her inclusion in any history of nineteenth-century French music.

Musical Examples
1. Scherzo from the Trio in E Minor
for Piano, Flute (or Violin), and Cello, op. 45
1862

Following a modified scherzo-trio form, which begins in a *vivace* tempo in E minor, this third movement presents a contrasting, slower trio in the parallel major. The scherzo itself is a virtuoso work which covers a wide range in both the piano and the flute parts, with one often imitating the other in detailed passage work.

There are few harmonic surprises in the scherzo, other than a smattering of augmented-sixth chords and a dissonant diminished seventh over clashing pedal point, marked *"sforzando,"* accompanied by trills in the flute and cello parts. A forté Neapolitan-sixth chord marks the beginning of the cadence pattern, closing the scherzo.

The trio, marked *Poco più sostenuto* and *doloroso,* moves in third-relation harmony from E major to G major and back again.

The repeat of the scherzo is almost exact, but the ending is innovative in that it recalls the main theme of the E major trio, then concludes with the scherzo theme in that key. The form, therefore, can be diagrammed as follows:

Scherzo	Trio	Scherzo
a:‖ba:‖	c:‖cd:‖	abca

The musical score for the complete trio is published by Da Capo Press (New York, 1979).

2. Adagio-Allegro
Fourth movement of Nonetto op. 38
1849

Premiered in November 1850 with the young violinist Josef Joachim, this work remains unpublished in spite of its many performances during Farrenc's lifetime. Scored for violin, viola, cello, double bass, flute, oboe, clarinet, bassoon, and French horn, the *nonet* is an unusual genre, rarely, if ever, used by women composers. The combination of winds and strings had been explored earlier by Farrenc in her symphonic overtures (1834) and her three symphonies (1841–1847). In this *nonet,* all nine instruments are blended together in a masterful way, perhaps reflecting the influence of her teacher, Anton Reicha.

The final movement, the Allegro, is preceded by a short, slow introduction of eight measures, based on dominant pedal point. When the Allegro begins, the melody is first presented in the violin, then in the flute. The few harmonic surprises are limited to shifts to the parallel minors and cadential use of the Neapolitan-sixth chord. A horn fanfare announces the Exposition's close in the dominant, and the ensuing Development section makes abundant use of imitation, fragmentation (of a three-note motive), and wandering modulations. The Recapitulation gives the melody to the clarinet, then to the oboe, and the harmonic surprises include deceptive cadences, plus the strategic use of the Neapolitan-sixth chord. Concluding in the tonic key, the codetta makes a passing reference to the subdominant key before ending the *nonet* with brilliant passage work.

The manuscript can be found at the Bibliothèque Nationale in Paris.

Selected List of Works
Piano

Variations on a Theme of Aristide Farrenc, op. 2 (1825)
Grand Variations, op. 4 (1825)
Variations on an Air of Rossini, op. 5 (1829–30)
Variations, op. 6 (1828)
Air Suisse Varié, op. 7 (1832)
3 rondos, op. 8 (1828)
Rondo brillant on a Theme of Bellini, op. 9 (1833)
Rondo brillant on a Theme of Onslow, op. 10 (1828)
Rondo brillant on a Theme of Weber, op. 11 (1833)
Variations on a Galopade, op. 12 (1833)
Rondo brillant on a Theme of Rossini, op. 13 (1833)
3 cavatines, op. 14 (1835)
2 melodies, op. 16 (1835–36)
Air Russe Varié, op. 17 (1835–36)
Rondo Valse, op. 18 (1836)
Fantasie and Variations, op. 19 (1837)
4 rondinos, op. 21 (1837)
Variations on a Theme of Count Gallenberg, op. 25 (1838)

30 études, op. 26 (1839)
Hymne Russe Varié op. 27 (1839)
Variations on a German Theme op. 28 (1839)
Variations on a Theme by Bellini, 4 hands, op. 29 (1839)
12 brillant études, op. 41 (1858)
20 études of medium difficulty, op. 42 (1865)
Mélodie, op. 43 (1858)
Scherzo, op. 47 (1858)
Valse brillante, op. 48 (1859–63)
Nocturne, op. 49 (1859–63)
25 easy études, op. 50 (1859–63)
Valse brillante, op. 51 (1864)

Orchestral

2 overtures, op. 23 and op. 24 (1834)
Symphony No. 1 in C minor, op. 32 (1841)
Symphony No. 2 in D major, op. 35 (1845)
Symphony No. 3 in G minor, op. 36 (1847)

Chamber

Variations on a Swiss Air, for piano and violin, op. 20 (1835–36)
Quintet in A Minor, for violin, viola, cello, double bass, and piano, op. 30 (1842)
Quintet in E Major op. 31 (1844–45)
Piano Trio in E♭ op. 33 (1850–55)
Piano Trio in D Minor op. 34 (1850–55)
Violin Sonata in C Minor op. 37 (1850–55)
Nonet in E♭ op. 38 (1849)
Violin Sonata in A Major op. 39 (1850–55)
Sextet in C Minor, for flute, clarinet, oboe, bassoon, horn, piano, op. 40 (1851–52)
Piano Trio in E♭ op. 44 (1861)
Trio in E Minor op. 45 (1862; Da Capo Press)
Cello Sonata in B♭ op. 46 (1861)

Books/Editions

Le Trésor des pianistes, 23 volumes (Paris, 1861–75; reprinted New York, 1978 [Da Capo Press] Bea Friedland, ed.)
Traité des abréviations (Paris, 1895)

Selected Discography

Piano pieces, op. 17 and 26: Musical Heritage 3766
Trio in D Minor, op. 34, no. 2, for piano and strings: Musical Heritage 3766
Piano Trio in E Minor for Flute, Cello, and Piano: Leonarda #104
Nonetto, op. 38, for chamber ensemble: Leonarda #110

Selected Bibliography

Friedland, Bea. *Louise Farrenc, 1804–75: Composer, Performer, Scholar.* Ann Arbor, MI: UMI Research Press, 1981.
——. "Louise Farrenc." In *Historical Anthology of Music by Women,* ed. James Briscoe. Bloomington, IN: Indiana University Press, 1987.
Gideon, Miriam. Introduction to Farrenc's *Trio in E Minor,* op. 45. Women Composers Series. New York: Da Capo Press, 1979.
The New Grove Dictionary of Music and Musicians, 1980 ed. S.v. "Farrenc, Louise," by Bea Friedland.

Louise Pauline Marie Héritte-Viardot

(1841–1919)

Musical Families

Biographical Summary

1841	Born in Paris, December 14, eldest child of Pauline Viardot-Garcia and Louis Viardot; niece of Maria Malibran.
Childhood	Studies voice with her mother.
1862	Marries Héritte, French consul-general of the Cape of Good Hope.
1862–86	Lives in both Paris and South Africa.
1886	Settles in Berlin, teaching singing.
1918	Dies in Heidelberg.

Not much information in English is available about the eldest daughter of Pauline Viardot-Garcia. In spite of the fact that she wrote her own memoirs and those of her family, in the history of women composers Héritte-Viardot has been eclipsed by her more famous mother. Although she was a performing contralto who wrote many songs and a renowned teacher of singing, she composed four string quartets, two piano trios, and a sonata for violin and piano—genres not often favored by singers. She also composed a comic opera entitled *Lindoro,* which was performed in Weimar in 1879, and a cantata, *Das Bacchusfest,* performed in Stockholm in 1880. Her teaching career took place in St. Petersburg, Frankfurt, Berlin, and Heidelberg.

Since so little information is available about her music or her musical career, it is difficult to place Héritte-Viardot in the tradition of late-nineteenth-century French music history. That she inherited much from the musical and literary background in which she grew up in the Viardot home in Paris may be reason enough for including her in the French musical tradition, but, like her mother, Héritte-Viardot composed in a style bearing little resemblance to that of her contemporaries Georges Bizet (1838–1875), Camille Saint-Saëns (1835–1921), Vincent d'Indy (1851–1931), or Gabriel Fauré (1845–1924).

In the following musical example, a Spanish rhythm pervades, suggesting the influence of her mother's family background and that of Héritte-Viardot's uncle, Manuel Garcia.

Musical Example
"Serenada" from Spanish Quartet *op. 11*
for Piano, Violin, Viola, and Cello
1883

This Serenada represents Héritte-Viardot the melodist. The ostinato-type piano part provides a Spanish dotted rhythm for the string instrument's spinning-out of essentially one long melody. Although a three-part form can be discerned, with a different instrument taking over the melody at the beginning of each section, there is very little, if any, attempt to write counter or contrasting melodies. A special effect occurs in the concluding section, when the piano presents the leading theme and the string instruments accompany it in pizzicato, imitating the Spanish guitar.

List of Works
Chamber

Quartet for piano, violin, viola, and cello (Boosey and Hawkes, 1883)
Spanish quartet for piano, violin, viola, and cello, op. 11 (Peters, 1883)
3 piano quartets
4 string quartets
2 piano trios
Sonata for violin and piano, op. 40 (Hofmeister, 1909)

Piano

In Gondola (Novello)
Serenade (Heugel)
Sonata for two pianos

Vocal

3 cantatas
Drei Lieder
Sechs Lieder
Several individual songs

Operetta

Comic opera in one act, *Lindoro* (1879)

Books

Memoires de Louise Héritte-Viardot (Paris, 1923)
Memories and Adventures (London, 1913; reprinted New York, 1978 [Da Capo Press])
Une famille de grands musiciens (1922)

Selected Bibliography

The New Grove Dictionary of Music and Musicians, 1980 ed. S.v. "Viardot, Pauline," by April Fitzlyon.

Cécile Chaminade

(1857–1944)

Chevalière de la Légion d'Honneure

Biographical Summary

1857	Born in Paris, into a nonmusical family of mariners, August 8.
1865	Composes her first pieces, church music.
1875	Piano debut in Paris.
	Concert tour of England and France, already performing her own compositions.
1888	Performance of her ballet, *Callirhoé*, in Marseilles.
1892	Appointed by the French government to the post of "Officer of Public Instruction."
1908	Makes her American debut, performing her *Concertstück* with the Philadelphia Orchestra.
1944	Dies in Monte Carlo on April 18.

The most prolific of the women composers discussed in this section, Cécile Chaminade composed over 350 works in a wide variety of genres: concerti, orchestral suites, a ballet, an opera, chamber music, a choral symphony, over 100 songs, and well over 200 piano pieces. Furthermore, most of her works enjoyed popularity during her lifetime, which, incidentally, was exceedingly long, spanning the last half of the nineteenth century and the first half of the twentieth. Most of her compositions were published during her lifetime by a number of distinguished firms: Enoch and Cie. and Durand, in Paris; B. Schott in Germany; J. Williams; Arcadia; and Hutchings and Romer in London; and the Anglo-Canadian Music Publishing Association in Toronto. Furthermore, shortly before her death the French government awarded her the title of Chevalière of the Legion of Honor.

But how is Chaminade's music remembered or evaluated today? Typically, the major music dictionaries label her piano music and songs as "salon music." Many of Chaminade's works in the smaller genres do fit into that tradition which was characteristic of much French music at the time. Salon pieces were intended for light entertainment, not for concert performance. A quick glance at the titles of some of Chaminade's piano pieces indicates a preference for the lighter genre: "La Lisonjera" ("The Flatterer"), "Valse caprice," "Autumn," "Pierrette," and her famous "Scarf Dance." Even some of the chamber works have descriptive titles: "Caprice de concert," "Chanson," "Trios morceaux," "Chant du nord," and "Danse orientale."

And yet, Chaminade composed larger works for the piano: a sonata, two sets of concert études, six pieces for piano and orchestra, and *Concertstück* for piano and orchestra, which she performed in America.

Such a prolific and successful composer need not be pigeonholed as a composer of salon music. After all, she enjoyed a fine and varied musical education, thanks to Hector Berlioz, who convinced her parents that the best possible musical instruction should be procured for their daughter. She studied piano with Felix Le Couppey (1811–1887); counterpoint, harmony, and fugue with Augustin Savard (1841–1881); violin with Martin Marsick (1848–1924); and composition with Benjamin Godard (1849–1895), who has also been labeled a composer of salon music, even though his output ran far outside the boundaries of the smaller, popular genres.

While salon music became the vogue in the latter half of the nineteenth century, not only in France but also in England and the United States, there was another style of composition developing in France, from which Chaminade should not be excluded. This "French Renaissance," as mentioned in the previous two essays, included such composers as César Franck, Camille Saint-Säens, Emanuel Chabrier, Henri Duparc, and Vincent d'Indy. Chaminade's songs, ballet, *Callirhoé,* and her ambitious choral work, *Les Amazones,* should be included in this style.

Paris concert audiences heard a great variety of music, to be sure. From 1861 to 1884, the "Concerts Populaires," directed by the French entrepreneur Jules Pasdeloup (1819–1887), premiered mostly orchestral and chamber music in his famous Sunday concerts, with an orchestra of over one hundred members. He consistently programmed works by contemporary French composers. Similarly, in keeping with the rising French nationalism of the 1870s, the "Concerts du Châtelet," originally the "Société Nationale," conducted by Eduard Colonne (1838–1910), introduced the French musical public to the compositions of their contemporaries, including Chaminade.

Perhaps the recent performances and recordings of Chaminade's larger genres, such as the *Concertino for Flute* or the *Concertstück for Piano and Orchestra*, will bring about renewed interest in her versatility in composing works other than salon music.

Musical Example
La Morena *op. 67*
a Spanish Caprice for Solo Piano

If a definition of salon music implies that the composer relies to a great degree on simple charm, then this particular example is one of salon music. Chaminade exhibits her gifts as a melodist in a most pleasing, simple way. Essentially, the piece is one of melody in the upper part and accompaniment in the lower part. The imitation of guitars occurs throughout, first in the rhythm of the lower part accompanying a Spanish-flavor melody, and then, more pronounced, in the middle section with fast repeated notes, strumming effects, rolled chords, and trills. The rapid changes in tempo, from lingerings and rubatos to agitated rushings forward, further characterize the emotional and expressive nature of this charming caprice. Essentially it follows the song form of *aba,* with a dramatic codetta.

Selected List of Works
Orchestra

Concertino, for flute and orchestra, op. 107 (1905)
Concertstück, for piano and orchestra, op. 40 (ca. 1896, pub. 1905)
2 orchestral suites
6 pieces for piano and orchestra, op. 55
2 pieces for orchestra, op. 79 (pub. 1925)

Chamber Music

2 piano trios, op. 11 and op. 34
Numerous pieces for violin and piano

Organ

Meditation

Piano

Over 200 pieces, including pieces for children *(Album des enfants,* op. 126); a *Symphonique* for two pianos, op. 117; concert études; arrangements of songs; and sonatas

Vocal

Approximately 100 songs
Les Amazones, op. 26, choral symphony (1890)

Ballet

Symphonic ballet for full orchestra and ballet, *Callirhoé* (1888)

Opera

Comic opera in one act, *La Sevillane* (1882)

Selected Discography

Piano pieces: EMI 2 C 069, 16410; EMI HQS 1287; Meridian E 77018; Gramophon DB 21183; Oiseau-Lyre DSLO 7; Orion ORS 7261; Musical Heritage 1139; Turnabout TV 34685; Victor 20346; Genesis GS 1024; Columbia D 13044; Victor 20346
Callirhoé, for ballet: Columbia 1658D & 9157; Decca 25189
Concertino, for flute and orch.: RCA ARL 1 3777
Concertino, for flute and winds: Avant AV 1015; RCA RL 2 5109
Concertino, for flute and piano: Award ASD 706
Concertstück, for piano and orchestra: Orion ORS 78296; Turnabout TV 34754
Etudes de concert, op. 35, for piano: EMI 2 C 069, 16410
Serenade espagnole, arrangement for violin and piano: Columbia 33027 D; Deutsche Grammophon 135133; Decca F 6179; Angel SZ 37630
Trio in G minor, op. 11, No. 1: Vox SVBX 5112

Selected Bibliography

Briscoe, James. "Cécile Chaminade." In *Historical Anthology of Music by Women,* ed. James Briscoe. Bloomington, IN: Indiana University Press, 1987.

The New Grove Dictionary of Music and Musicians, 1980 ed. S.v. "Chaminade, Cécile," by Gustave Ferrari and Jean Mongredien.

Lili Boulanger

(1893–1918)

The Prix de Rome

Biographical Summary

1893	Marie-Juliette Olga (Lili) born into Parisian musical family, August 21. Her father, Ernest (b. 1815), taught voice at the Paris Conservatory, and her mother, Raissa, born in Russia, was a singer; her older sister, Nadia (b. 1887), was to become one of the most famous teachers of composition in the twentieth century.
1895	Suffers a severe case of bronchial pneumonia, which leaves her susceptible to many illnesses during the rest of her life.
1898	Death of her baby sister.
	Audits harmony classes of Auguste Chapuis (1859–1933) with her sister at the Paris Conservatory.
1899	Audits organ classes of Louis Vierne (1870–1937), her sister's teacher at the Conservatory.
	Sight-reads songs by Gabriel Fauré to her sister's piano accompaniment.
1900	Death of her father, a sudden shock to Lili.
1901	First public performance as a violinist.

	Attends composition classes of Fauré's assistant, André Gédalge (1856–1926).
1902	Attends organ classes of Alexandre Guilmant (1837–1911).
	Attends composition classes of Gabriel Fauré at the Conservatory.
1904	First public performance as a pianist.
	Sister Nadia's final exams from the Conservatory, temporarily halting Lili's auditing classes.
1905	Family moves to 36 rue Ballu in Paris, where other notable musicians lived, namely, Georges Caussade (1873–1936), who later taught Lili at the Conservatory, and Paul Vidal (1863–1931), who also taught Lili at the Conservatory in 1912.
	Lili, in poor health, is sent to various spas in Frankfurt, Lausanne, Geneva, Interlaken, and Zurich.
1905–9	Sporadic musical study, but intensive reading program at home, initiated by Lili, including the Greek classics as well as French Symbolist poets.
1907	Composes 2 psalms for soloist and orchestra (Psalm 131 and 137).
1908	Composes an Ave Maria for voice and organ.
1909	Composes 2 more psalms for chorus and orchestra (Psalm 1 and 119).
	Completes a setting of I Corinthians, chapter 13, for chorus and orchestra.
	Becomes proficient on the cello and harp, in addition to the violin and piano.
1909–11	Begins formal lessons in harmony, counterpoint, and composition with George Caussade and Paul Vidal.
1911–13	Intense period of study, of composing, and of preparing for the Prix de Rome contest, between intermittent bouts of ill health. More than 16 works composed during this time. Summers spent with family and artist-musician friends at Hannecourt and/or Gargenville.
1913	In seclusion at the Palace of Compiègne for the final round of composing for the Prix de Rome, May 22–June 21. Other contestants include the composers Claude Delvincourt (1888–1954) and Marcel Dupré (1886–1971).

	Awarded the first prize, Prix de Rome, for her cantata *Faust et Hélène* (July 5).
	Signs an exclusive contract with the Italian publishing firm Ricordi in August.
1914	Takes up residency in the spring at the Villa de Medici in Rome to compose, as part of the Prix de Rome award; returns to Paris during outbreak of World War I.
1914–16	Joining the war effort, she works for a humanitarian organization, helping drafted musicians and their families.
1916	Returns to the Villa de Medici, but illness forces her to return to France.
1916–18	Composes 7 works, the last 2 of which are dictated from her sickbed: "D'un soir triste" and "Pie Jesu," for voice, string quartet, harp, and organ, her last composition.
1918	Dies at age 25.

Plagued most of her short life by an illness that would have been diagnosed and treated today as Crohn's disease, Lili Boulanger composed over fifty works in the ten years between the time she decided to become a composer, 1908, and the year of her early death, 1918. Although she worked in a wide variety of genres, her main contributions are in sacred and secular vocal music: works for chorus with and without orchestra, vocal chamber works, songs, cantatas, and one unfinished opera. Perhaps she is best known for the cantata that won her the Prix de Rome in 1913, *Faust et Hélène*. Other winners during the contest's 110-year history included Hector Berlioz (1803–1869), Georges Bizet (1818–1893), Jules Massenet (1842–1912), Claude Debussy (1862–1918), Gustave Charpentier (1860–1956), and Lili's father, Ernest Boulanger (1815–1900), who won the prize in 1835.

Lili Boulanger, then, inherited a rich French musical tradition, of which she became a link in the chain, often being compared to the impressionist composers Debussy and Maurice Ravel (1875–1937). She grew up in the most sophisticated of musical and artistic circles. Among her father's close friends were the composers Charles Gounod (1818–1893) and Massenet, the organist and composer Théodore Dubois (1837–1924), and many other notable musicians who taught with him at the Paris Conservatory.

Even after her father's death, when Lili was seven years old, Lili's mother, Raissa Boulanger, continued to cultivate the friendship of creative artists both in the family apartment in Paris and in the Boulanger's summer residence in Gargenville. Among the family friends during the first decade of the twentieth century were such diverse talents as the well-known violinists Eugene Ysaye (1858–1931) and Jacques Thibaud (1880–1953), the Dutch conductor Wilhelm Mengelberg (1871–1951), the pedagogue and composer Paul Vidal (1863–1931), the Italian novelist and poet Gabriele d'Annunzio (1863–1938), the pianist and art collector Raoul Pugno (1852–1914), and the organist and director of the Conservatory Théodore Dubois. Indeed, the friends and acquaintances of the Boulanger family, both before and after the death of Ernest Boulanger, represented the elite of French artistic and intellectual society of that era. This was a most stimulating atmosphere for the two sisters, Nadia and Lili Boulanger.

Boulanger's musical education, though sporadic because of her ill health, was entrusted to the best teachers from the Paris Conservatory. Auditing classes that Nadia attended, the young Boulanger's early exposure to the organ class of Louis Vierne and the composition class of Gabriel Fauré was to leave a lasting impression on her. It was in Fauré's class that she met and became friendly with many known composers of this century: Alfredo Casella (1883–1947), Charles Koechlin (1867–1950), Georges Enesco (1881–1955), Florent Schmidt (1870–1958), and Maurice Ravel. Before long, Gabriel Fauré became a frequent visitor in the Boulanger home, as did Paul Vidal, who was to become Lili's teacher in 1912, helping her to prepare for the Prix de Rome, which he had won in 1883 for his cantata *Le Gladiateur*.

Also among her early teachers were Fernand Luquin (violin), Hélène Chaumont (piano), and Fernando Reboul (cello). When she officially became a composition student at the Conservatory, in 1909, all lessons were privately arranged through her principal teachers, Georges Caussade and Paul Vidal. She was tutored intensively in counterpoint, fugue, and composition in order to prepare for the Prix de Rome competition.

The contest required that the entrants go into seclusion in order to compose a fugue on a given subject and a cantata on a given text. As ill health continued to plague Boulanger throughout the final round of the contest and the required residency at the Villa de Medici in Rome, not a few critics misunderstood the special attention she required: she could not be left alone, requiring assistance in managing everyday tasks (the other contestants remained in seclusion).

Nevertheless, Boulanger did win the Prix de Rome, and a month later signed a contract with the prestigious Italian publishing firm of Ricordi. Her compositions began to appear on programs in both Europe and the United States.

To mainstream Lili Boulanger into French music history of the early twentieth century is to invite comparison with Claude Debussy and the impressionist composers. This is not without some validity, as many of her works utilize impressionist techniques: preference for text settings of symbolist poets, an emphasis on subtlety and understatement, occasional use of exotic subjects, and melodies and harmonies that focus on whole-tone and pentatonic scales. Her two favorite symbolist poets were Maurice Maeterlinck (1862–1949) and Francis Jammes (1868–1938); it was on the poetry of Jammes that Boulanger composed her song cycle *Clairières dans le ciel*. Other writers whose texts she set included Charles-Jean Grandmougin (1850–1930)—*Les Sirènes;* Casimir Delavigne (1793–1843)—*Hymne au Soleil;* and Alfred de Musset (1810–1857)—*Pour les funérailles d'un soldat.*

Perhaps what is most impressionistic is Boulanger's very sparing use of any *forte* or *fortissimo* dynamic level. There is always that suggestion of uncertainty, perhaps even regret or melancholy, perhaps due to her prolonged state of ill health.

But Boulanger also inherited a neo-Romantic style, similar to that of the music of Gabriel Fauré, Marcel Dupré (1886–1971), or Charles-Marie Widor (1844–1937). Boulanger's early works tend to emphasize chromaticism and contrapuntal textures, more characteristic of romanticism than of impressionism.

Considering her lifelong battle with sickness and depression, Boulanger's compositional output is truly astounding. That she managed to compose so much of such high quality before her death at age twenty-five is as remarkable as are her first-class musical skill and her musical imagination.

Even though France was in the midst of war at the time of Boulanger's death in 1918, the Parisian press took considerable notice of her death. As a further tribute, conductor Walter Damrosch programmed several of her works in New York in 1918, and in February 1919, the U.S. journal *The Musician* honored her with a two-column obituary. The publishers Durand and Ricordi published many of her later compositions posthumously.

Musical Examples
1. Nocturne for Flute and Piano
1912

The piano accompaniment of this short piece provides a steady, almost ostinato rhythm for a beautiful melody spun out by the solo flute. Although not impressionistic in its harmonic vocabulary, it is typical of Boulanger's preference for understatement in dynamic level and avoidance of melodic cadence. The flute part is not virtuosic, though it does make use of scale passage work as it progresses to the first long-awaited cadence of a high *C*. This tonal nocturne is accessible for listeners and performers alike.

2. D'un matin de printemps
("A Spring Morning")
for Flute and Piano
1918

This version of *D'un matin de printemps,* written for either flute or violin, is one of the last pieces Boulanger wrote in her own hand, some months before her death. Unlike the sacred compositions of her last two years, this is atypically marked *gai, léger* ("gaily, lightly"). Animated, highly rhythmic, and virtuosic in its demands on both flutist and pianist, this work exhibits a recognizable formal structure in its sectional repetitions. Its musical language is representative of the French style at the turn of the century, with its emphasis on parallelism, on open fifth and fourth intervals, and on modal melodies and harmonies. The quick tempo and the reiteration of rhythmic chords in the accompaniment propel the work forward in a type of perpetual motion, further atypical of Boulanger's late compositional style.

Selected List of Works
Choral

2 psalms: 131 and 137 (1907)
2 psalms: 1 and 119 (1909)
I Corinthians, chapter 13 (1909)
Apocalypse (1909)
Les Sirènes, for mezzo soprano, chorus, and piano (1911)
Soleil de septembre (1912)
Le Soir, for chorus and piano (1912)
Hymne au soleil, for chorus and piano (1912)

Chorus and Orchestra

La Tempête (1913)
Soir sur la plaine (1913)
Psalm 24, for organ, chorus, and orchestra (1916)
Psalm 129, for baritone, male chorus, and orchestra (1916)
Du fond de l'abîme, for organ (1914–17)
D'un matin de printemps, symphonic poem (1917)

Vieille prière bouddhique (1917)
D'un soir triste, symphonic poem (1918)

Opera

La Princesse Maleine (unfinished; Maeterlinck, 1918)

Cantatas

Frédégonde (1913)
Faust et Hélène (1913)

Vocal Chamber

Pie Jesu, for mezzo soprano, string quartet, harp, and organ (1918)

Songs

La Lettre de mort (1906)
Attente (Maeterlinck, 1910)
Reflets (Maeterlinck, 1911)
Le Retour (G. Delaguys, 1912)
Clairières dans le ciel (F. Jammes)

Orchestral

Piece for trumpet and small orchestra (1915)
Sicilienne, for small orchestra (1916)
Marche gaie, for small orchestra (1916)
Marche funèbre (1916)
Poème symphonique (1917)
D'un soir triste (1918)

Piano

5 études (1909)
3 études (1911)
Variations (1914)
D'un jardin clair (1914)
D'un vieux jardin (1914)

Chamber

Nocturne for violin and piano (1911)
Nocturne for flute and piano (1912; G. Schirmer)
Piece for oboe and piano (1914)
Cortège, for violin or flute and piano (1914)
Sonata for violin and piano (1916)
D'un matin de printemps, for flute and piano (1918; Durand and Cie.)

Selected Discography

Clairières dans le ciel: Spectrum SR 126; Leonarda #118
Cortège, for violin and piano: RCA ARM 4 0942; Vox, SVBX 5112
Du fond de l'abîme, for choir and orchestra: Everest LPBR 6059; Everest SDBR 3059
D'un matin de printemps, for flute and piano: Leonarda #104; Musical Heritage 4339
Faust et Hélène, for choir and orchestra: Vox SVBX 5112
Nocturne, for violin and piano: Columbia 4872; Decca M 570; Vox SVBX 5112
Pie Jesu, for voice and orchestra: Everest LPBR 6059; Vox PLP 6380; Turnabout TV 4183
Pour les funerailles d'un soldat, choir and orchestra: Vox SVBX 5112
Psaume 24, for choir and orchestra: Everest SDBR 3059
Psaume 129, for choir and orchestra: Everest SDBR 3059
Vieille prière bouddhique, for choir and orchestra: Everest SDBR 3059

Selected Bibliography

The New Grove Dictionary of Music and Musicians, 1980 ed. S.v. "Boulanger, Lili," by Dominique Jameux.
Rosenstiel, Léonie. "Lili Boulanger." In *Historical Anthology of Music by Women*, ed. James Briscoe. Bloomington, IN: Indian University Press, 1987.
——. *The Life and Works of Lili Boulanger*. Madison, NJ: Fairleigh Dickinson University Press, 1978.

Amy Marcy Cheney Beach

(1867–1944)

U.S. Symphonist

Biographical Summary

1867	Born to Charles Abbott Cheney, a paper manufacturer, and Clara Imogen Marcy Cheney, a pianist and singer, in Henniker, New Hampshire on September 5, an only child.
1871	Begins composing simple waltzes.
	Family moves to Boston.
1873	Begins formal piano instruction with her mother, 3 lessons a week.
	Attends a small private school in Boston. Studies piano with Ernst Perabo (1845–1920), Junius Hill (1840–1916), and Carl Baermann (1839–1913).
1881–82	Studies harmony with Junius Hill, the only formal instruction in music theory she would ever have.
1883–85	Debuts with the Boston Symphony, performing the Moscheles Piano Concerto in G Minor.
1885	March: Performs again with Boston Symphony, playing Chopin's Piano Concerto in F Minor.
	Marries prominent Boston surgeon, Dr. Henry Harris Aubrey Beach, 24 years her senior, on De-

	cember 2. From then on, she concentrates on composition.
1889	Begins work on her Mass in E♭.
1891	Serves on piano awards committee of the New England Conservatory, along with Arthur Foote (1853–1937) and Edward MacDowell (1860–1908).
1892	Premiere of her Mass in E♭, by the Handel and Haydn Society in Boston, February 7. Well received, with standing ovation, but it was not performed again until 1984, in New York.
	On the same evening, Beach performs the piano part in Beethoven's *Choral Fantasy.*
	Winter: New York Symphony Orchestra, under conductor Walter Damrosch, performs her *Eilende Wolken,* op. 18, for alto soloist and orchestra. The first work by a woman to be performed by the Symphony Society of New York.
	Commissioned to write *Festival "Jubilate"* for the Women's Building of the World Columbian Exposition.
1896	Premiere of her *Gaelic Symphony,* op. 32, by the Boston Symphony.
1897	January: Six weeks after completing the *Gaelic Symphony,* she writes the Sonata for Violin and Piano, op. 34, which she performs with Franz Kniesel (1865–1926) at one of his quartet concerts.
1898	March: Appears in a program of her own works to benefit the Elizabeth Peabody House in Boston.
1900	Premiere of her last big orchestral work, the *Piano Concerto in C♯ Minor* op. 45, dedicated to pianist Teresa Carreño, by the Boston Symphony.
1910	Death of her husband of 25 years.
1911–14	Moves to Europe, where she tours, playing her concerto and other works in Hamburg, Leipzig, Rome, and Berlin. Her symphony is also performed in Leipzig and Berlin.
1914	Settles in New York City, making concert tours, composing, and spending summers at either Cape Cod or the MacDowell Colony.
1931	Her *Canticle of the Sun* op. 123, for chorus and orchestra, performed at the Worcester Festival and then at several New York churches.
1932	Composes her only opera, *Cabildo,* at age 65.

1933	Receives medal from the Chicago International Exposition, for creative work in music.
1938	Composes her *Piano Trio in A Minor* op. 150, at age 70.
1940	Honored at a dinner in New York's Town Hall Club, attended by over 200 musicians, composers, and friends.
1941	Composes her last work, "Though I Take Wings of Morning," on a text from Psalm 139.
1944	Dies in New York City on December 27, age 77, of heart disease.

Amy Beach is a remarkable woman in the history of late-nineteenth- and early-twentieth-century U.S. music, in that her compositions in the larger genres of symphony, mass, and concerto were performed widely by major orchestras both here and abroad, especially in the years between 1893 and 1914. Beach is one of the first U.S. women composers to have achieved such prominence.

For the most part self-taught in musical composition, Beach never studied in Europe, as did most of the male composers of her generation. Perhaps she never wanted to study abroad, as she had already debuted as a pianist with the Boston Symphony by the age of sixteen. Two years later she married a prominent Boston surgeon, thus making European study an impossibility.

Her musical gifts, combined with first-class craftswomanship, earned her great respect and popularity during her lifetime. As of 1940, only 3 of her 150 opus numbers remained unpublished, and this in itself is a remarkable record for any American composer. Furthermore, beginning around 1920, Amy Beach clubs began springing up all over the country, as local music teachers came to admire her songs and piano pieces. Her songs were perhaps the most popular of her works, and she is reputed to have bought a summer home in Cape Cod solely on the royalties of her three songs, op. 44 (1899), on Robert Browning texts: "Ecstasy," "Ah, Love, but a Day," and "The Year's at the Spring."

A gifted pianist and composer, Amy Beach enjoyed a privileged position in Boston society, which permitted her to work unencumbered by financial worries. From an early age, her mother, a pianist and singer, encouraged her daughter in not only piano but musical composition. She later studied under the best piano teachers in Boston, though she actually took less than one year of formal instruction in harmony, with Junius Hill. She taught herself counterpoint and fugue, by writing out from memory much of Bach's *Well-Tempered Clavier*, then comparing her version to Bach's. She taught herself orchestration by reconstructing from memory themes she had heard at concerts, comparing them to the original score. Her piano teacher, Ernst Perabo, had been a student of Ignaz Moscheles and Carl Reinecke in Leipzig, and her other piano teacher, Carl Baerman, a student of Franz Liszt. From all sides, then, she absorbed the grand tradition.

The music public and the critics were, for the most part, encouraging and enthusiastic. Her marriage to Dr. H. H. A. Beach provided her with over twenty-five years of moral and monetary support. Dr. Beach was an amateur musician himself and a personal friend of prominent Bostonians, including the writer and physician Oliver Wendell Holmes.

The Boston Symphony performed her works, and the publishing firms of Arthur Schmidt Co., C. C. Birchard and Co., and Oliver Ditson Co. faithfully brought out her newest compositions. After her husband's death in 1910, and her touring in Europe (1910 to 1914), when she settled in New York City, three New York publishing firms became interested in, and eventually published, her music: G. Schirmer, H. W. Gray & Co., and the Composers' Press. Indeed, Amy Beach enjoyed such favorable circumstances all her life that she never had to teach to earn money. The only conflict she admitted to was that of being a performing artist versus a composer. Since hers was a childless marriage, Amy Beach was free to pursue both performance and composition throughout her life.

To mainstream Beach in the history of American music is not without its problems. If and when she is mentioned in music history textbooks, she is usually assigned a place in the late-nineteenth-century and turn-of-the-century "Boston" or "New England" school, founded by the composer-teacher John Knowles Paine (1839–1906). The leading composers of the New England group included George Chadwick (1854–1931), Arthur Foote (1853–1937), Horatio Parker (1863–1919), and, perhaps, Edward MacDowell (1860–1908). Although these New Englanders wrote in U.S. idioms, the fact remains that U.S. music was dominated by European compositions and models. All of the New England composers except Foote studied in Europe, and the U.S. concert halls and opera houses were dominated by European repertory.

Beach never studied composition with any of the New England school composers, and her self-directed study focused on the European masters. She admitted to a preference for Richard Wagner and Johannes Brahms, and it is true that her early chromatic style often resembles that of the late-nineteenth-century German composers.

Although she was probably not affected by the compositional style of the U.S. women composers who preceded her, she surely benefited from their acceptance and moderate popularity in nineteenth-century America. Those women, who wrote in the accepted genres of parlor music, hymns, or sentimental ballads, include Augusta Browne (1821–1882), Faustina Hasse Hodges (1823–1895), Jane Slonam (b. 1824), and Mrs. E. A. Parkhurst (1836–1918). Composing within their own limited spheres, these women had their music performed and published during their lifetimes, making way for gradual acceptance of U.S. women composers working in larger genres.

During her lifetime, Amy Beach was a close friend of the musician and patron Marian MacDowell, to whom she dedicated her *Three Piano Pieces,* op. 128. It was at the MacDowell Colony in Peterborough, New Hampshire, that Amy Beach met and befriended two women composers, somewhat younger than she. Mabel Daniels (1878–1971) and Mary Howe (1882–1964) were inspired by Beach to carry on the legacy of U.S. women composing in the early part of this century. These two women, like Beach, composed in the larger genres of symphony, opera, and concerto, with some success.

Other U.S. women composers followed in close succession. In the last quarter of the nineteenth century, women had gained entry into the nation's conservatories of music. At first they had only been permitted to study as performers, but by the turn of the century women were admitted to composition classes. With publishers like A. Schmidt of Boston interested in publishing their music, a generation of U.S. women composers won some distinction. These include Mary Carr Moore (1873–1957), the black composer Florence Price (1888–1944), Marion Bauer (1889–1955), and the conductor-composer Ethel Leginska (1886–1970). Beach's success certainly encouraged these women to compose in the larger genres. One other contemporary of Beach was Margaret Ruthuen Lang (1867–1972). Her *Dramatic Overture,* op. 2, was performed by the Boston Symphony under Arthur Nikisch, in April 1893, three years before its performance of Beach's *Gaelic Symphony.*

It is interesting that Amy Beach never espoused any kind of feminist ideas regarding women composers' due place in the concert repertoire. As early as 1898 she turned down an offer to write about women in music, saying she was too busy composing. In 1915 she proudly stated that she never felt limited because she was a woman. And yet, after the 1900 premiere of her *Piano Concerto in C# Minor* op. 45, written at age thirty-two and dedicated to the virtuoso pianist Teresa Carreño, Beach rarely wrote in the larger genres of orchestral music. In the next forty-four years she continued writing songs, piano pieces, chamber music, two cantatas for soloists, orchestra, and chorus, an opera, and a lengthy piano trio, but there were to be no more masses or concerti, or symphonies similar to the ones that had won her such recognition. In the 1920s and 1930s Beach wrote a considerable amount of church music. A devout Episcopalian all her life, she composed numerous anthems, a motet for a cappella chorus, a *Service in A Major* op. 63, a Te Deum, and the two cantatas.

Her name remained before the U.S. public as long as she lived; she received many honors from clubs and societies and an Honorary Master of Arts degree from the University of New Hampshire in 1928. In 1933, when she was awarded a medal from the Chicago International Exposition, she was still considered one of the leading American composers. For a while, music critics linked her with the descendants of the New England school, particularly with John Alden Carpenter (1876–1951).

And yet her musical style is eclectic, reflecting aspects of Brahms, Wagner, MacDowell, and perhaps even Debussy. Typical of the late Romantic period, her larger works exhibit lush chromaticism, many altered chords, broadly spun-out melodies, involved development of themes, and complex harmonies. Her songs, now considered sentimental, rely on a natural gift for melody, but with piano accompaniments rarely simplified.

Musical Example
Excerpts from Quartet for Strings, *op. 79*
(later classified as op. 89, by Beach)
1929

In a concert honoring the composer's seventy-fifth birthday, in 1942, this quartet was given its official premiere. This is one of Beach's three unpublished works. It is also her only string quartet.

The work is highly chromatic, but with impressionist undertones. The first section opens with a two-chord motive which evolves into a rather long, slow introduction to the more rhythmically active section. This middle section develops into a fugato, which doesn't last long before three more pizzicato chords announce the last section. There is a return to the slow, reflective, almost impressionistic mood of the first section. The piece ends in an ethereal atmosphere, with chromatic harmonies supporting very long melodies. One wishes that Beach had once again tried her hand at composing string quartets, but it was not to be.

Selected List of Works
Opera

Cabildo op. 149 (1932)

Orchestral

Gaelic Symphony in E Minor op. 32 (1896)
Piano Concerto in C# Minor op. 45 (1899)

Chorus and Orchestra

Mass in E♭ op. 5 (1891)
Festival Jubilate op. 17 (1892)
The Chambered Nautilus op. 66 (1907)
The Canticle of the Sun op. 123 (1925)
Christ in the Universe op. 139 (1931)

Chamber Music

Sonata for violin and piano, op. 34 (1896)
Piano quintet in F# minor, op. 67 (1908)
Variations for flute and string quartet, op. 80 (1920)
Quartet for strings, op. 79 (1929)
Piano trio in A minor, op. 150 (1938)
3 other pieces for violin and piano

Piano

4 pieces, op. 15 (1892)
Scottish Legend op. 54 (1903)
Variations on a Balkan Theme op. 60 (1904)
4 Eskimo pieces, op. 64 (1907)
Suite française, op. 65 (1905)
From Blackbird Hills op. 83 (1922)
Fantasia fugata op. 87 (1917)
By the Still Waters op. 114 (1932)
Tyrolean Valse fantasie op. 116 (1924)
Out of the Depths op. 130 (1932)
18 other pieces
3 pieces for 4 hands

Songs

4 songs, op. 1 (1885–87)
3 songs, op. 19 (1893)
2 songs, op. 26 (1894)
3 songs, op. 37 (1897)

Amy Marcy Cheney Beach   153

5 Burns songs, op. 43 (1899–1900)
3 Browning songs, op. 44 (1899)
4 songs, op. 56 (1904)
2 songs, op. 77 (1913–15)
2 songs, op. 100, with violin and cello obbligato (1932)
2 songs, op. 131 (1932)
Though I Take the Wings of Morning, op. 152 (1941)
Approximately 120 others
Vocal duets

Other Choral

50 unaccompanied choral pieces
Eilende Wolken for alto and orchestra, op. 18 (1892)

Selected Discography

Piano pieces: Genesis GS 1054; Northeastern Records 204; Turnabout TV 34685; Musical Heritage 3808 and 4236
Songs: Composers Recordings, Inc. (CRI) SD 462; Seraphim 60168; His Master's Voice, HQM 1190; New World 247; Victor 87026; London OS 26537
Concerto, op. 45, for piano and orchestra: Turnabout QTVS 34665
Pastorale, woodwind quintet: Musical Heritage 3578
Quintet for F# Minor, op. 67, for piano and strings: Turnabout TVS 34556
Sonata in A Minor, op. 34, for violin and piano: New World 268
String Quartet, op. 79: Leonarda #111
Symphony in E Minor, op. 32: Society for the Preservation of American Music MIA 139
Theme and Variations, op. 80, for flute and string quartet (Gaelic): Leonarda #105
Trio, op. 150: Vox SVBX 5112

Selected Bibliography

Ammer, Christine. "New England's Lady Composers." In *Unsung. A History of Women in American Music.* Westport, CT: Greenwood Press, 1980.
Block, Adrienne Fried. Introduction to *Amy Beach: Quintet for Piano and Strings in F Sharp Minor, op. 67.* Women Composers Series. New York: Da Capo Press, 1979.

——. "Amy Marcy Beach." In *Historical Anthology of Music by Women,* ed. James Briscoe. Bloomington, IN: Indiana University Press, 1987.

Glickman, Sylvia. Introduction to *Amy Beach: Piano Music.* Women Composers Series. New York: Da Capo Press, 1982.

Neuls-Bates, Carol. "A Corollary to the Question: *Sexual Aesthetics in Music Criticism,* 1820–1920." In *Women in Music.* New York: Harper & Row, 1982.

The New Grove Dictionary of Music and Musicians, 1980 ed. S.v. "Beach, Amy Marcy Cheney," by Judith Tick.

Notable American Women, A Biographical Dictionary, ed. Dena Epstein. S.v. "Beach, Amy Marcy Cheney." Cambridge, MA: The Belknap Press of Harvard University Press, 1971.

Tick, Judith. "Passed Away Is the Piano Girl: Changes in American Musical Life, 1870–1900." In *Women Making Music,* ed. Jane Bowers and Judith Tick. Chicago: University of Illinois Press, 1986.

Rebecca Clarke

(1886–1979)

English Performer and Composer

Biographical Summary

1886	Born in Harrow, England, into a musical family on August 27.
1894	Begins studying violin with Hanns Wesseley, from the Royal Academy of Music.
1903	Begins composing songs.
1907	Begins to study composition with Sir Charles Stanford (1852–1924) at the Royal College of Music; counterpoint and fugue with Sir Frederick Bridge (1844–1924); and viola with Lionel Tertis.
1912	Joins the Queen's Hall Orchestra, becoming one of the first women members of a professional orchestra in London.
1913–15	Founds an all-woman piano quartet, the English Ensemble, which tours England, and a member of a women's string quartet.
1916	Comes to the United States, where she establishes herself as a composer and viola soloist.
1919	Wins second prize at the Berkshire Music Festival at Tanglewood in Massachusetts, for her *Sonata for Viola and Piano*.

1921	Again wins second prize at the Berkshire Festival for her important work, the *Trio for Violin, Cello and Piano*.
1923	Returns to London and tours Europe with the English Ensemble.
1929	Writes entries on the viola and on Ernst Bloch for Cobbett's *Cyclopedic Survey of Chamber Music* (1929).
1944	Marries pianist James Friskin (1886–1967), settles in New York City, and begins touring the world with him, playing viola and piano solo recitals and chamber music.
1945f.	Teaches and lectures at the Chautauqua Institute, New York; hosts a weekly radio program about chamber music.
1979	Dies in New York City.

Spanning three-quarters of the twentieth century, the life and works of Englishwoman Rebecca Clarke exemplify some of the musical trends and opportunities that have been opened to women during this century.

As a concert violist, Clarke toured the world, playing chamber music with such notables as Pablo Casals (1876–1973), Jacques Thibaud (1880–1953), Artur Rubinstein (1886–1982), Jascha Heifetz (b. 1901), Artur Schnabel (1882–1951), and pianist James Friskin (1887–1967), her husband. In 1919, her viola sonata tied with Ernst Bloch's *Suite for Viola and Piano* in the chamber music competition established by Elizabeth Sprague Coolidge at the Berkshire Festival in Massachusetts. All entries for the contest were anonymous, and when the distinguished jury asked that Mrs. Coolidge cast the final vote to break the tie, the first prize of $1,000 went to Ernst Bloch. Nevertheless, when the second-prize winner was announced, everyone was astonished to see that she was a woman. Clarke won second prize in the same competition two years later for her *Piano Trio* (1921).

Clarke, unlike Amy Beach, had formal education, at the Royal College of Music, and enjoyed the privileges of being admitted to classes in composition, counterpoint, and fugue. Some of her renowned teachers included: Sir Charles Stanford (1852–1924), composer of over two hundred songs, symphonies, operas, and chamber music, and Sir Frederick Bridge (1844–1924), organist and composer of numerous choral works. Her viola teacher, Lionel Tertis, encouraged her not only to perform and tour but also to compose for her instrument.

Clarke also wrote several important articles for music journals and encyclopedias during the 1920s. These include articles on the Beethoven quartets, on the history of the viola in string quartet literature, published in the English journal *Music and Letters,* on Ernst Bloch, and on the viola for W. W. Cobbett's *Cyclopedic Survey of Chamber Music.*

She had little trouble finding publishers for her music in England and in the United States. Her main publishers in London were Winthrop Rogers and the Oxford University Press; in the United States, G. Schirmer published much of her chamber music.

Although she is known mostly for her chamber music, particularly the larger prize-winning works (the *Viola Sonata* and the *Piano Trio*), Clarke wrote over fifty-eight songs and part-songs. Solo songs were her earliest compositions, dating from 1903 to 1907, before she entered the Royal College of Music for formal study. In fact it was the early songs, on texts by Goethe, Maurice Maeterlinck, Rudyard Kipling, and Richard Dehmel, that won her a place as the first female student in the composition class of Sir Charles Stanford, the teacher of the notable English composer Ralph Vaughn Williams (1872–1958). The songs that Clarke composed during her student years at the Royal College of Music favored English musical themes and texts by William Shakespeare, William Butler Yeats, and William Blake.

Sometime after the composition of her viola sonata, Clarke adopted the pseudonym Anthony Trent. In a 1976 interview on the occasion of her ninetieth brithday, Clarke admitted that those compositions submitted to publishers under the male pseudonym received more attention and acclaim than those submitted under her real name. One of the reasons for this regrettable circumstance may be that from 1923 on, Clarke was known as a concertizing violist. It may also be that the publishers reacted differently when they thought the composer was male rather than female.

During those two decades between 1923 and her marriage in 1944, Clarke composed over twenty instrumental or chamber works. In England she may have been known for a few short years as Anthony Trent, but in the United States she was Rebecca Clarke. In August 1942, she was the only woman among more than thirty composers present at the International Society for Contemporary Music (ISCM) in San Francisco. Her *Prelude, Allegro, and Pastorale* for clarinet and viola was enthusiastically received and reviewed.

But her composing career was to come to an almost complete halt after her marriage to and subsequent tours with pianist James Friskin. Whether she chose to devote herself to touring as a viola-piano team with her husband, or whether marriage directly curtailed her career as composer remains unclear. At any rate, Clarke left the music world an impressive catalogue of works before her marriage at the age of fifty-eight.

To mainstream Clarke into the music history of the first half of the twentieth century invites comparison with her fellow countrymen Ralph Vaughn Williams or Gustav Holst (1874–1934). Certainly much of her music sounds English in its frequent use of English folk tunes, along with the modal harmonic framework within which the tunes are cast. In the early twentieth century, English nationalism was in vogue among those composers trained at the Royal College of Music. However, Clarke's instrumental works of the 1920s and the early 1930s may show a kinship with the musical style of Maurice Ravel (1875–1937) and Ernest Bloch (1880–1959), both of whom she knew well, worked with, and admired.

Two other English composers may have contributed to Clarke's musical heritage. They are Sir Edward Elgar (1857–1934), whose music, firmly rooted in nineteenth-century Romanticism, came into prominence from 1890 to 1900, and Dame Ethel Smyth (1858–1944), whose orchestral works, mass, and operas were performed in London, also in the 1890s and the first quarter of the twentieth century. Smyth's musical activities received considerable attention between 1908 and 1930 in London. Although German-educated, Ethel Smyth certainly helped pave the way for Clarke's acceptance as a woman composer in England.

Musical Example
from the Trio for Violin, Cello, and Piano
"Allegro Vigoroso," the third movement
1921

This is the trio that won second prize at the Berkshire Festival in 1921. Its first public performance following the competition took place in November 1922 at Wigmore Hall in London, with Dame Myra Hess (1890–1965) at the piano. It was published six years later by Winthrop-Rogers in London.

In this lively finale, Clarke uses English country dance themes along with transformations of the motto theme from the first movement. Frequently the harmony is modal, in keeping with the English folk song tradition. However, when the counterpoint becomes very involved, the implied harmony is dissonant, sometimes verging on the bitonal. The movement is high-spirited, exhibiting a rhythmic vitality and a clarity of melodic development that exemplifies a composer of considerable craftswomanship and inventiveness.

The musical score of this trio is published by Da Capo Press.

Selected List of Works
Songs with Piano

Approximately 50 songs and part-songs (1920–25) including:
  The Aspidistra
  The Cherry Blossom Wand
  The Cloths of Heaven (Yeats)
  Cradle
  Down by the Salley Gardens (Yeats)

Sacred, Vocal

Psalm for a cappella chorus (1920)
Psalm for voice and piano (1920)

Piano

Cortège

Chamber Music

Approximately 24 instrumental chamber works, including:
  Sonata for viola and piano (1919)
  Piano trio (1921; Boosey and Hawkes)
  Chinese Puzzle, for violin and piano (1922)
  Grotesque, for viola and cello (1918)
  Lullaby, for viola and cello (1918)
  Midsummer Moon, for violin and piano (1924)
  Passacaglia on an old English Tune, for viola and piano (1943)
  Rhapsody for cello and piano (1923)
  Suite for clarinet and viola (1942)
  Two pieces for viola or violin and cello (1930)

Selected Discography

Sonata for Viola and Piano: Supraphon 111 2694
Trio for Violin, Cello, and Piano: Leonarda #103
Viola and Chamber Music (5): Northeastern NR 212

Selected Bibliography

Bernstein, Jane A. "Rebecca Clarke." In *Historical Anthology of Music by Women,* ed. James Briscoe. Bloomington, IN: Indiana University Press, 1987.

Sherman, Robert. Interview with Rebecca Clarke in New York City in 1976, on the occasion of her ninetieth birthday, as recorded on Leonarda Sampler Cassette, vol. 1.

PART FIVE

Six Living U.S. Composers

Katherine Hoover

(b. 1937)

Virtuoso Flutist and Composer

Biographical Summary

1937	Born in Elkins, West Virginia, into nonmusical family.
1940	Family moves to Philadelphia.
1947	Begins studying flute in school.
1952	Begins piano study.
High School	Receives mediocre music instruction.
1955–57	Enters academic program, University of Rochester, New York.
1957–59	Studies at Eastman School of Music; studies flute with Joseph Mariano; receives Performer's Certificate in flute and Bachelor of Music degree in theory.
1960–61	Studies flute with William Kincaid in Philadelphia.
1961–67	Teaches flute at the Juilliard School of Music, Preparatory Department.
1965–66	First performance of one of her compositions, *Duet for Two Violins*.
1969–84	Teaches flute and theory at Manhattan School of Music.

1972	First publication of one of her compositions: *Three Carols,* by C. Fischer, Inc.
1973	Receives Master's degree in Music Theory from Manhattan School of Music.
1978–81	Originates and organizes festivals of women's music in New York City.
1981	Commissioned by the Episcopal Diocese of New York, her *Psalm 23* is performed by a chorus of 400 with orchestra in New York's Cathedral of St. John the Divine.
1987	Premiere of her work for full orchestra, *Eleni: A Greek Tragedy,* by the Harrisburg Symphony in February.
	Qwindtet, commissioned by the Hudson Valley Wind Quintet, premieres at the Women in Music conference at the State University of New York, New Paltz in April.
	Lyric Trio performed at the Spoleto Festival, Charleston, South Carolina, in May.
	Clarinet Concerto premieres in September, by clarinetist Eddie Daniels with the Santa Fe Symphony, New Mexico.
	In celebration of Hoover's 50th birthday, Robert Sherman's WQXR radio program "The Listening Room" is dedicated to performances of her compositions, November 30.
1988	"Kirby International," a cable television program in New York, features interviews with and performances by Hoover, January.
	Performance of *Eleni: A Greek Tragedy* by the Classical Symphony of Chicago, May.
1986–present	Teaches graduate students in flute and composition at Columbia University Teacher's College.

A composer in a wide variety of genres, from orchestral, choral, and chamber music to works for solo instruments and solo voice with instruments, Katherine Hoover is also a performing concert artist, an accomplished flutist. But because of prejudice she encountered against woman majoring in composition at the undergraduate level, Hoover's academic degrees are in music theory.

Growing up in a nonmusical family that discouraged her from majoring in music in college, Hoover entered a standard academic program at the University of Rochester, transferring to the Eastman School of Music in her junior year. The impetus to compose didn't occur until several years after her college graduation and after establishing herself as a flutist and teacher in New York. In 1966, her *Duet for Two Violins* was performed in New York, and for the first time Hoover considered composing to be part of her future. Six years later Carl Fischer, Inc., published her first composition, *Three Carols*.

Since that time, Hoover has been the recipient of a National Endowment for the Arts composer's grant, awards from the American Society of Composers, Authors, and Publishers (ASCAP) and other organizations, as well as numerous commissions. Many of her works have been published by Theodore Presser, Carl Fischer, and Boelke Bomart, and have been recorded on the Leonarda label. Among the performers who have presented her works are the Dorian and Sylvan Wind Quintets, the Alard Quartet, the Atlanta Chamber players, the Huntington Trio, and the New York Concerto Orchestra. More recently, a portion of her *Medieval Suite* (1983–84) was used on the Public Broadcasting System's "The Artist Was a Woman," which was nationally broadcast, and her *Homage to Bartók* (1975), a woodwind quintet, was recently chosen to be broadcast on the BBC.

Hoover is also an impresario, whose organization and supervision of the Festivals of Women's Music in New York City from 1977 to 1981 produced not only a reawakening of interest in women's music but also the taping and subsequent broadcasting of the work of over fifty-five historical and contemporary women composers. It was a pioneering effort of major significance. Hoover has chronicled her experiences as the festivals' organizer in an article in *The Musical Woman,* volume 2 (Greenwood Press, 1987). Some of her comments are offered here, as they help illuminate the difficulties and rewards of such an undertaking.

> The concerts were, as usual, musically rewarding and underattended. There was very little publicity, despite the hiring of a better-known public relations firm. Again, I took artists and composers for an appearance on "The Listening Room" with Robert Sherman, and gave a short interview on WNCN. There was a review in *The New York Times* which was very helpful to one composer, but totally ignored the rest of the program. Thirteen new composers were represented. [P. 354]

Regarding the music critics' reactions to the four festivals, Hoover offers this insight:

> Obviously critics vary widely in their outlooks and perceptions. . . . Most of these [prejudices] are, I think, the result of a conviction that if any of this material were worthy, they, as experts, would know of it after so many years in the field. Indeed, it is a mark of the sad, twisted history

of women's compositions that so many scholars and critics don't know of them. [P. 358]

And as to the overall organization and conception of the festival, Hoover admits that the production of the festivals was largely due to her own dedication and enormous efforts:

> In terms of planning and direction, the Festivals were largely a one-person effort. The Women's Interart Center was indispensable in many respects. . . . WIC has a reputation for impressive artistic success and an equal reputation for administrative problems. WIC provided the opportunity for these festivals and gave me a free hand and much encouragement . . . but it also undermined them by disorganizing my plans because of serious confusions, lack of deadlines, frequent changes of personnel, and fiscal mismanagement. [P. 359]

Nevertheless, the festivals disseminated women composers' music that had been, until then, either unheard or ignored. Performances, recordings, broadcasts, and exposure in the media all added up to a plus, as Hoover reflects: "We have reached, literally, millions. . . . Despite the bitterness of debt, it is an experience I shall always remember with gratefulness, fatigue, and pride in all concerned" (p. 362).

Hoover has now turned her efforts to "75% composing and 25% performing," as commissions are quickly coming her way. She likes to refer to herself as "an old performer and a new composer." With the premiere performance of her work for full orchestra, *Eleni: A Greek Tragedy,* by the Harrisburg Symphony in February 1987, and with the issuing of three new compact discs on the Leonarda label, Hoover is fast emerging as a major talent in twentieth-century American music composition.

Musical Example
From Divertimento for Flute and Strings
Conclusion of the first movement, Allegro giocoso, *through second movement,* Adagio-Vivace
1975

Hoover has commented about this spirited and inspired work:

> The *Divertimento* is, as its name implies, a light work, and one that was written with the enjoyment of the performers much in mind. It is a "flute quartet," using the flute as a substitute for the first violin in the traditional string quartet. The musical sources are international—French, a touch of Russian, a bit of jazz. The fast section of the second movement has short "character" motifs for each instrument, which are sometimes

played alone, sometimes mixed, rather like individual steps in an exuberant country dance. [Hoover, jacket notes for *Music for Flute and String by Three Americans,* 1980, Leonarda Productions, #105]

Perhaps one of her most popular pieces, the *Divertimento* has received favorable reviews from numerous music critics. The following comments are cited in promotional material supplied by the composer:

> It is entertaining work distinguished by its skillful mixing and matching of texture and timbre, and its clever instrumental effects. [June Schneider, *The Atlanta Record]*

> Hoover's *Divertimento* . . . is a work with tougher fiber, making the flute the leader of the quartet. Its tangy harmonic base gives the work an agreeable vigor. [Daniel Webster, *The Philadelphia Inquirer]*

> The *Divertimento* deserves a welcome place not only in the flutist's repertoire, but also in the history of American music. [Thomas Warner, *American Music]*

The *Divertimento* is, indeed, a charming and enjoyable work, finely crafted and exhibiting skillful treatment of all the instruments. That Hoover herself is a virtuoso flutist is evident here, but the richly varied style is characteristic of much more. It represents a major American composer whose present dedication to composition promises much for the future.

List of Works
Chamber Music for Instruments

The Medieval Suite, for flute and piano (1979–81; Theodore Presser)
Trio for violin, cello, and piano (1978)
Sonata for brass quintet (1985)
Lyric Trio, for flute, cello, and piano (1983)
Divertimento, for flute, violin, and cello (1975; Papageno Press)
Images, for cello, violin, and piano (1981)
Qwindtet op. 37 for wind quintet (1987)
Homage to Bartok, for wind quintet (1975)
Suite for Saxophones, for soprano, alto, tenor, and bass saxes (SATB) (1980)
Sinfonia, for 4 bassoons (1976)
Serenade, for cello and string quartet (1982)
Aria, for cello or bassoon and piano (1982–85)
Suite for Two Flutes (1977–81; Boelke-Bomart)
Duo for Flutes (six simple duets) (1982; Boelke-Bomart)

Trio for Flutes (1974)
Allegro giocoso, for cello and piano (with aria) (1985)

Solo Instrumental Music

Reflections, for flute (1982)
Set for Clarinet (1978; Boelke-Bomart)
Piano Book
    Chase (1977)
    Lament (1977)
    Three plus Three (1977)
    Allegro molto (1978)
    Forest Bird (1980)
    Poem (1981)
    Dream (1982)
Andante and Allegro, for piano, medium student level (1983)

Solo Voice with Instruments

From the Testament of François Villon, for bassoon-baritone, bassoon, string
    quartet (1982)
Selimar, for soprano clarinet, piano (1979)
To Many a Well, for mezzo or soprano and piano (1977)
Lullay, Lullay, for soprano, piano (1971)
Wings, for soprano, flute, clarinet, violin, piano (1974)
Seven Haiku, for soprano, flute (1973)
Four Carols, for soprano, flute (1970)

Orchestra

Eleni: A Greek Tragedy op. 36 (1986; Presser)
Clarinet Concerto op. 38 (1987; Presser)
The Medieval Suite, for orchestra (1983–84; Presser)
Summer Night op. 34, for flute, horn, strings (1985; Presser)
Psalm 23, SATB chorus and small orchestra (1981)
Nocturne, for flute, strings, percussion (1977)
Summer Night, for flute, horn, strings (1985)
Eleni: A Greek Tragedy, full orchestra (1986)

Choral Music

The Last Invocation (Whitman) SATB (1984)
Sweet Thievery (Hoover) (1985)
Songs of Celebration, SATB and keyboard or brass quintet (1983; Lawson-
   Gould)
Christmas
Songs of Joy, SATB and keyboard or brass quintet (1974, Carl Fischer)
Psalm 23, for SATB and organ (1981)
Three Carols, for 2 sopranos, alto, and flute (Christmas 1972; Fischer)
Four English Songs, SATB, oboe, English horn, piano (1976)
Syllable Songs, SSA, woodblock (1977)
Canons, voices and lengths variable (1972–73)

Discography

The Medieval Suite, op. 18: Leonarda #121
Reflections, op. 25: Leonarda #121
Piano Trio, op. 14: Leonarda #103
Lyric Trio, op. 27: Leonarda #325
Divertimento for Flute, Violin, Viola and Cello, op. 7: Leonarda #105
Images, op. 22: Leonarda #326
Summer Night, op. 34: Leonarda #327
Sinfonia for 4 Bassoons: Leonarda #102

Selected Bibliography

Hoover, Katherine. "Festivals of Women's Music." *The Musical Woman,* vol.
   2, ed. Judith Zaimont. Westport, CT: Greenwood Press, 1987.

To contact the composer, write to:
The American Music Center
250 West 54th Street, Room 300
New York, NY 10019

Ellen Taaffe Zwilich

(b. 1939)

The Pulitzer Prize

Biographical Summary

1939	Born in Miami, Florida, on April 30.
1944	Begins studying piano. Would later study violin and trumpet.
1949	Begins composing, writing down music.
High School	Concertmistress of school orchestra; first trumpeter in school band.
1961	Bachelor's degree in music, Florida State University.
Graduate School	Master's degree in music, Florida State University. Major teachers: John Boda and Carlisle Floyd.
1964	Moves to New York City, as freelance violinist. Studies violin with Richard Burgin and Ivan Galamian.
1965–72	Plays violin in the American Symphony Orchestra under Leopold Stokowski. Marries Joseph Zwilich, violinist in the Metropolitan Opera Orchestra.
1974	Awarded the Elizabeth Sprague Coolidge Chamber Music Prize.
1975	Awarded a gold medal in the 26th annual Inter-

national Composition Competition, in Vercelli, Italy.

First woman to receive doctorate in composition from the Juilliard School. Major teachers: Roger Sessions and Elliott Carter.

1979   Sudden death of Joseph Zwilich.

1982   Performance of her *Passages* for soprano and chamber ensemble at the Edinburgh Summer Festival.

1983   First woman to receive the Pulitzer Prize in music composition, for her *Symphony No. 1 (Three Movements for Orchestra)*.

1984   *Celebration for Orchestra* commissioned and premiered by the Indianapolis Symphony Orchestra.
Double Quartet for Strings commissioned and premiered by the Chamber Music Society of Lincoln Center.
Concerto for Trumpet and Five Players commissioned and performed by the Pittsburgh New Music Ensemble.

1985   *Symphony No. 2* ("Cello Symphony") commissioned and premiered by the San Francisco Symphony. *Concerto Grosso 1985* commissioned and performed by the Washington Handel Festival Orchestra.

1986   Receives the Arturo Toscanini Music Critics Award for New World Recording of *Symphony No. 1, Celebration for Orchestra,* and *Prologue and Variations for String Orchestra.*
Concerto for Piano and Orchestra commissioned by the American Symphony Orchestra League and the Detroit Symphony Orchestra; premieres at Meadow Brook Festival.
Images for Two Pianos and Orchestra commissioned by the National Museum of Women in the Arts, and premiered at museum's opening by the National Symphony Orchestra.

1987   *Trio for Violin, Cello, and Piano* commissioned by the Kalichstein-Laredo-Robinson Trio.
Tanzspiel, a ballet in four scenes, commissioned by the New York City Ballet.

1988   Performances in the spring of Piano Trio in San Francisco, Los Angeles, Chicago, New York City, and Washington, D.C.

New York City Ballet's premiere of *Tanzspiel*.
Praeludium for organ premieres by James Christie, at the American Guild of Organists' annual meeting in Boston.
Symbolon, an orchestral work, premieres by New York Philharmonic; tours Leningrad and Moscow.
Commission from Chicago Symphony Orchestra for pair of works for trombone and orchestra.
Currently living in New York City.

The first woman to receive the Pulitzer Prize in Music Composition, in 1983 for her *Symphony No. 1,* Ellen Zwilich has composed in a wide variety of genres, although she is perhaps best known as a composer of instrumental music. Her music has been widely performed both in the United States and in Europe, and she has been the recipient of many prizes, awards, and commissions. Unlike most twentieth-century composers, Zwilich now makes her living solely as a composer, unaffiliated with any university or teaching institution. This, in itself, is a remarkable achievement, considering how difficult and rare it is to live principally from grants, cash awards, commissions, performances, and royalties. But Zwilich, a widow who lives in a one bedroom apartment in the Bronx, has recently been able to do just what she enjoys most—compose.

She began composing at a very early age, possibly around the time she started piano lessons at age five, although she didn't write down any of her pieces until a few years later. Although Zwilich's family was not musical, they encouraged their daughter in her musical pursuits of playing the violin, piano, and trumpet and composing. What is most unusual about Zwilich is that even in elementary school, she knew that she wanted to become a composer.

As a high school violinist, she was concertmistress of the school orchestra and was first trumpeter of the band. At Florida State University, while majoring in composition, she played jazz trumpet and violin and sang in the Collegium Musicum. As a student composer, much of what she wrote was performed by the University Orchestra. By the age of twenty-two, Ellen Zwilich had already enjoyed the privilege, mostly reserved for composition professors on university faculties, of experiencing the public performance of many of her works.

After she moved to New York City in 1964, supporting herself as a freelance violinist, Zwilich continued to compose, even though she was principally active as a performer. When she joined the American Symphony Orchestra as a violinist, she had the opportunity to play under such distinguished conductors as Leopold Stokowski, the orchestra's founder, Ernest Ansermet, Karl Boehm, and André Previn. She also played under such contemporary composer-conductors as Luciano Berio, Aram Khachaturian, and Hans Werner Hense. Of her seven-year tenure in the orchestra, Zwilich comments: "I was already aware that I wanted to compose more than I wanted to play. Composers need some kind of hands-on experience, either as conductors or players." And, continuing about the importance of composers spending time as apprentice performers, a situation that has been noted in most of these essays, Zwilich asserts: "My experience as a performer has certainly shaped the way I think about music and what I think about composing. What is paramount in my mind is the concept of how a piece is going to work in performance" *(New York Times,* July 14, 1985).

In the late 1960s, Ellen Taaffe married Joseph Zwilich, a violinist in the Metropolitan Opera Orchestra. In 1970, she entered the Juilliard School as a doctoral candidate in composition, where she had the privilege of studying with two of America's leading composers, Roger Sessions and Elliott Carter. Of their influence on her, Zwilich remarks: "They were immensely helpful in my development. They allowed me my independence, the best thing you can say about a teacher. I don't think my music sounds at all like either of them, but they influenced my thinking irrevocably." *(New York Times,* July 14, 1985)

In 1975, Zwilich graduated from The Juilliard School of Music, the first woman in the history of the school to be awarded a doctorate in composition. Performances of her works in New York City were well under way when, in the mid-70s, Pierre Boulez premiered her *Symposium for Orchestra.* Fellowships, awards, and premieres followed, and everything seemed to be going well for Zwilich when, suddenly, in 1979, her husband died of a heart attack during a performance in his own place of employment, the Metropolitan Opera House.

At the time of her husband's death, Zwilich was writing her *Chamber Symphony.* When she finally returned to finishing it, she realized that:

> Everything had changed. . . . Suddenly all talk of method and style seemed trivial. I wanted to say something, musically, about life and living. . . . We've had to come to grips with an incredible amount of evil and pain in this century . . . , but this agony is only one reality; we shouldn't forget beauty, joy, nobility, and love—greater realities which artists must learn to express once again. [*New York Times,* July 14, 1985]

Her *Chamber Symphony,* written in Joseph Zwilich's memory, has become one of her most performed works, following its premiere with the Boston Musica Viva under the direction of Richard Pittman. The following press comments are cited in the promotional materials supplied by the composer's manager. Of the *Chamber Symphony*'s premiere, two Boston critics observed: "The Chamber Symphony made a direct appeal to near-traditional notions or coherence, sentiment, and instrumental beauty" (Richard Buell, *The Boston Globe*), and "The Chamber Symphony was decidedly romantic" (Ellen Pfeiffer, *Boston Herald American*).

Critics tend to group Zwilich with the neo-Romantic composers of this century, as can be seen in Andrew Porter's review of her Pulitzer Prize–winning *First Symphony*: "[The First Symphony] is an unabashedly romantic composition, lushly Straussian in sound, enjoyable to hear" *(The New Yorker)*.

Whatever is meant by "unabashedly romantic" or "enjoyable to hear," Zwilich's music is neither abstract nor without audience appeal. Perhaps the critic Donal Henahan has best summed up Zwilich's ability to communicate through her art. Of the premiere of her *Double Quartet for Strings* by the Chamber Music Society of Lincoln Center, Henahan wrote: "This was a composer intent on communication with her audience, and in full command of the technical means to do so. . . . Zwilich displayed a clear-eyed maturity and a rare sense of balance. She unites music that pleases the ear and yet has spine." *(New York Times, 1984)*.

Most present-day composers find themselves, at some time or another, explaining how the composing process works for them, or how a particular work came into being, or how they view the evolution of their style. Zwilich has been interviewed a number of times about all of these aspects of her own artistic creativity. In general, she composes in the morning, after music has been running through her head all night. She begins with a large number of sketches, themes, suggested harmonies, structures, dramatic ideas, and a vague idea of the form. Then she adds to these ideas, improvising on the piano and violin. According to Zwilich, "Inspiration engenders product, which, in turn, engenders more inspiration . . . but it must *sound*" *(New York Times)*. Further elaborating on the way critics have labeled her "a romantic," Zwilich explains: "I'm not really a wide-eyed romantic. . . . I do a lot of thinking before I begin a new work . . . but then once I'm writing, something mysterious happens . . . once you're into a new work [you] let it take you somewhere you've never been before" *(New York Times, July 14, 1985)*.

Reviewing her *Concerto for Piano and Orchestra*, music critic Robert Croan wrote: "She is one of the more significant living American composers . . . the new concerto is continuing proof that it is possible to compose aurally pleasing new music without sacrificing a 20th-century identity" *(Pittsburgh Post-Gazette, 1986)*.

Her music is clearly accessible and yet of first-class craftswomanship. Her career is one of the most remarkable twentieth-century success stories in the history of U.S. women composers.

Musical Examples
The third and fourth songs from the cycle Einsame Nacht *("Lonely Night"), on poems by Hermann Hesse*
1971

According to the composer, these particular poems are concerned with existential loneliness. "Yet while themes of homesickness, alienation, and loss are explored, there is a wonderful life-affirming sensuousness and immediacy in the poetry. . . . One experiences, with Hesse, a recognition of the isolation of the human condition together with a profound yearning for connection" (record jacket notes by Alan Hershowitz, *Songs of American Composers,* Leonarda #120).

Translation of Texts

Schicksal ("Destiny")

In our fury and muddle
We act like children, cut off,
Fled from ourselves,
Bound by silly shame.

The years clump past
In their agony, waiting,
Not a single path leads back
To the garden of our youth.

Elisabeth ("Elizabeth")

I should tell you a story,
The night is already so late—
Do you want to torment me,
Lovely Elizabeth?

I write poems about that,
Just as you do;
And the entire history of my love
Is you and this evening.

You mustn't be troublesome,
And blow these poems away.
Soon you will listen to them,
Listen, and not understand.

The musical setting of both poems is dramatic, perhaps more so in the piano accompaniment than in the solo voice (bass baritone). The piano part encompasses a wide range, and there are frequent alternations between voice and piano commentary. *Schicksal* begins with a fast-paced introduction, but the middle and last sections are somewhat more understated. In *Elisabeth,* the dynamic level is subdued, and the tempo is slow throughout, in keeping with the melancholy nature of the poem.

List of Works
Orchestra

Symposium for Orchestra (1973; Merion Music)
Passages (orchestral version) (1982; Margun Music)
Symphony No. 1 (Three Movements for Orchestra) (1982; Margun)
Prologue and Variations for String Orchestra (1983; Merion)
Celebration for Orchestra (1984; Merion)
Symphony No. 2 (1985; Merion)
Concerto Grosso (1985; Mobart Music Publications)
Concerto for Piano and Orchestra (1986; Merion)
Images for Two Pianos and Orchestra (1986; Merion)
Tanzspiel, ballet in four scenes (1987; Merion)

Solo, Chamber, and Ensembles

Sonata in Three Movements, for violin and piano (1973–74; Merion)
String Quartet (1974; Margun)
Clarino Quartet, for 4 trumpets or 4 clarinets (1977; Margun)
Chamber Symphony (1979; Merion)
Passages (1981; Margun)
String Trio (1982; Merion)
Divertimento, for flute, clarinet, violin, and cello (1983; Mobart)
Fantasy for Harpsichord (1983; Mobart)
Intrada (1983; Margun)
Prologue and Variations for String Orchestra (1983; Merion)
Double Quartet for Strings (1984; Merion)
Concerto, for trumpet and 5 players (Merion)
Trio for Piano, Violin, and Cello (1987)
Praeludium for organ (1987; Mobart)

Vocal

Einsame Nacht, song cycle for baritone and piano on poems by Hermann Hesse (1971; Merion)

Emlékezet, for soprano and piano (1978), on Hungarian poems by Sándor Petöfi

Im Nebel, for contralto and piano (1972), on German poem by Hermann Hesse

Trompeten ("Trumpets"), for soprano and piano (1974), on German poem by Georg Trakl, English translation by the composer

Passages, for soprano solo and chamber ensemble (also in orchestral version) (1981; Margun)

Chorus

Thanksgiving Song (1986; Merion)

Discography

Symphony No. 1 (Pulitzer Prize): New World NW 336
Prologue and Variations for String Orchestra: New World NW 336
Celebration for Orchestra: New World NW 336
Chamber Symphony: Cambridge CRS 2834
String Quartet (1974): CRS
Sonata in Three Movements for Violin and Piano: CRS
Passages, for soprano and instrumental (Ensemble String Trio): Northeastern Records 218
String Trio: Northeastern Records 218
Prologue and Variations for String Orchestra: New World NW 336
Song Cycle, Einsame Nacht: Leonarda #120

Selected Bibliography

LePage, Jane Weiner. "Ellen Taaffe Zwilich." *Women Composers, Conductors, and Musicians of the Twentieth Century,* vol. 2. Metuchen, NJ, and London: The Scarecrow Press, 1983.

The New Grove Dictionary of American Music, H. Wiley Hitchcock and Stanley Sadie, eds. London and New York: Macmillan Press, 1986. S.v. "Zwilich, Ellen Taaffe," by James G. Roy, Jr.

Page, Tim. "The Music of Ellen Zwilich." *New York Times Magazine,* July 14, 1985, p. 26–30.

Terry, Ken. "Ellen Taaffe Zwilich." *B.M.I.: The Many Worlds of Music* (1983): 46–47.

Zwilich, Ellen, with Bruce Creditor. "Ellen Taaffe Zwilich." In *Historical Anthology of Music by Women,* ed. James Briscoe. Bloomington, IN: Indiana University Press, 1987.

To contact Zwilich's concert manager, write to:
Music Associates of America
224 King St.
Englewood, NJ 07631
(att: Mr. George Sturm)

To contact the composer, write to:
The American Music Center
250 W. 54th St. (Rm. 300)
New York, NY 10019

Ruth Schonthal

(b. 1924)

Emigré Composer and Teacher

Biographical Summary

1924	Born in Hamburg, Germany, to Viennese parents, June 27.
Childhood	Studies piano at the Stern Conservatory in Berlin.
1934	Family moves to Stockholm to escape Hitler.
1937	Publication of *Piano Sonatina*.
1937–40	Studies at the Royal Academy of Music, Stockholm.
1941	Sudden departure from Sweden in January, three months before graduation from the Royal Academy, as all Scandinavian countries are occupied by the German army. Three-month odyssey to Mexico, via Moscow, the Trans-Siberian Railroad, boat trips from Vladivostok to Japan to Mexico.
1942	Marries Oscar Ochoa.
1943	Birth of first son.
1944	Divorce from Oscar Ochoa.
1944–46	Studies composition with Ernesto Halffter and Manuel M. Ponce, a former student of Paul Dukas.
	Studies piano at the National Conservatory of Mu-

sic, with Pablo Castellanos, a student of Edwin Fischer.

Piano concert at the Palacio de Bellas Artes, the result of winning first prize in a piano contest. Some of her own compositions are included on the program.

Performance of two large orchestral works at the palace.

Supports herself by playing in nightclubs in Mexico City.

1946	Travels to the United States to study with Paul Hindemith, at Yale University, on scholarship.
1950	Graduates from Yale (Bachelor's degree in composition). Marries Paul Seckel, an artist.
1950–54	Plays piano in cocktail lounges. Teaches piano privately in Westchester County, New York.
1954	Birth of second son.
1958	Moves to Westchester; birth of third son.
1962	Becomes acquainted with composer Paul Creston. Publication of *Miniatures* by Shawnee Press.
1970	Publication by Oxford University Press of four works.
1970s	Teaches at Adelphi University and New York University, part-time: theory, composition, ear training, piano.
1979	Joins the faculty of Westchester Conservatory, teaching composition, piano, theory, form, and analysis.
	Begins teaching piano and composition students at home, and working with public school music teachers, White Plains, New York.
1980	Finalist in New York Opera Competition, for *The Courtship of Camilla*.
	Nominated for Friedheim Prize in Composition, Washington, D.C.
1981	Receives Certificate of Merit from Alumni Association of Yale University School of Music, for distinguished service in music.
1983	Returns to Germany as guest of mayor of Berlin. *Reverberations,* for prepared piano, chosen to be performed in "Education for Peace through Music" programs in German schools.

1984–present	Returns to Germany annually.
	Frequent appearances as guest panelist on New York radio broadcast "First Hearing," WQXR.
1988	Premiere of *The Young Dead Soldiers,* a work for chorus and orchestra, Cologne, Germany.

The only foreign-born contemporary composer considered here, Ruth Schonthal lived and worked in several different countries before coming to the United States in 1946. In spite of the many interruptions in her musical career, beginning with her family's exile from Nazi Germany in 1934 which led her to Stockholm, Moscow, and finally Mexico in 1941, Schonthal has managed to compose a large amount of music in a wide variety of genres. Included among the "interruptions" is a history of personal and family problems that resulted in the continual necessity to earn money and to be a caretaker. Schonthal surmounted these problems, and today she is recognized not only as a versatile composer but also as a concert pianist, a frequent lecturer and panelist, and an accomplished teacher.

While living in Germany before Hitler came to power, Schonthal was accepted, at the age of five, as the youngest pupil at the Stern Conservatory in Berlin, where she studied piano and music theory until 1934. Continuing her studies at the Royal Academy of Music in Stockholm, Schonthal composed a piano sonatina that was published when she was thirteen. When the family arrived in Mexico in 1941, Schonthal married at the age of sixteen and shortly thereafter gave birth to her first son. When the marriage dissolved, Schonthal, living with her parents, began studying composition with Ernesto Halffter, who soon introduced her to the Mexican pianist and composer Manuel Ponce, a former student of the noted French composer Paul Dukas. Ponce gave her a scholarship to study with him, and he introduced her to his circle of friends, including the renowned performers Andrés Segovia, Henryk Szeryng, and Gyorgy Sandor. During that time, Schonthal enrolled in the National Conservatory of Music in Mexico City, where she continued piano studies with Pablo Castellanos, a student of Edwin Fischer. Very soon she became well known as a performing pianist, and by age nineteen she had even composed two large orchestral works: *Six Preludes for Orchestra* and *Concerto Romantico* for piano and orchestra, both of which were performed in Mexico.

During the early years in Mexico City, Schonthal earned money by playing popular cocktail music at night. She learned a given number of new tunes every day, improvising on them, but also improvising her own mood music.

Her big break occurred when the composer Paul Hindemith came to Mexico to conduct several concerts. After hearing the young Schonthal perform her own sonatina and the second movement of her piano concerto in a private audition, Hindemith offered her a scholarship to study with him at Yale University. In the fall of 1946, Schonthal went to New Haven. Of her famous teacher she writes:

> The first year with Hindemith was not very creative for me. Whereby I thought of the whole texture moving forward, he thought of a single strand bending each original idea according to a strictly organized aesthetic. [Letter to the author, September 1986]

In New Haven, again having to support herself, Schonthal continued playing cocktail music, but now added classical music to the repertoire she performed in the Yale Law School dining room. Here she met her future husband, Paul Seckel, a student at the art school. In 1950 they married.

Again to earn money, Schonthal became the cocktail lounge pianist of New York's Hotel Shelbourne. She assumed the stage name of Carmelita, in homage to her Mexican second home. Even though the job left her days free for composing, Schonthal slowly started to resent the shallowness of the music she played to earn a living; it began to infiltrate her musical mind. By the time her second son was born, in 1954, and her first son had come to live with her in New York, Schonthal again sought other means of employment. She decided to devote herself to private teaching, taking the train from New York City to Westchester County, going from house to house five or six days a week.

The family moved to Westchester in 1958, and she opened her own private studio, teaching as many as forty-five students a week. However, in her private piano teaching, she became isolated from the musical-creative world. As Schonthal writes, "My animo [sic] for creativity was at a low point. I started many things without finishing them, which is one of the sure-fire ways of killing inspiration" (letter to the author, September 1986).

Actually, when she did find time to compose, Schonthal's musical style was seemingly at odds with the dictums of the day. After graduating from Yale, her aesthetic goals had been to write music as beautiful as the "old music in the European tradition." Isolated as she was, she continued to compose in this style. In 1962, she became acquainted with the composer Paul Creston, who not only encouraged Schonthal but also introduced her to many of his musical friends. It was during this period that she composed what she considers her best works, the *String Quartet 1* and the *Totengesänge*.

Creston introduced her to Shawnee Press which soon published her piano *Miniatures,* volumes 1 and 2, originally written for children. They were later re-issued by Galaxy Press, with volume 3 added. It was at this time that Schonthal finally joined ASCAP, the American Society for Composers, Authors, and Publishers.

In 1970, Oxford University Press made plans to publish many of Schonthal's works. However, after four publications, they dropped the project, naturally a great disappointment to the composer. Having just joined the faculty of Adelphi University on Long Island, Schonthal immersed herself in teaching, initiating such courses as "Insight into Music" for nonmusic students. She accepted an offer to teach at New York University, where she was given the opportunity to teach music composition (in addition to theory, ear training, composition, group piano, and private piano).

At both Adelphi and New York universities, Schonthal was employed part-time. Another job change was in order, which came in the form of conservatory teaching. At the Westchester Conservatory, Schonthal has taught composition, piano, theory, form, and analysis. At the time of this writing, she remains on the faculty at the Westchester Conservatory, additionally teaching private students at home, a few gifted composers among them.

How has she been able to compose? Schonthal admits, "It has been a tremendous struggle to find time and energy to compose, copy, contact artists, having to spend so much time earning a living" (letter to the author, September 1986).

Schonthal's caretaking and financial responsibilities have not diminished with the passing of time. Yet, in spite of these burdens, she has received considerable recognition as a composer. For her one-act opera, *The Courtship of Camilla,* Schonthal became a finalist in the 1980 New York Opera Competition. The previous year, she had been nominated for the Kennedy Center Friedheim Award for her set of twenty-four piano preludes, *In Homage Of. . . .* For the string quartet discussed below, Schonthal was awarded a Delta Omicron International Prize in 1962. She has received many ASCAP awards and has frequently appeared in colleges and universities in "meet the composer" programs.

Since the summer of 1983 Schonthal has returned yearly to her native Germany, as composer, pianist, lecturer, and panelist. Her music has been performed in the United States as well as in London, Glasgow, Paris, Belgrade, Mexico City, and various cities in Australia on radio and television. In addition to her recognition as composer, teacher, and pianist, Schonthal is well known for her lectures and workshops and as panelist, critic, and adjudictor. At the time of this writing, she is completing a textbook on the teaching of music composition in the private studio. Her audience? The home-based music teachers who want their young students to learn many aspects of music and music theory, through the creative art of composing.

Musical Example
String Quartet, *concluding sections*
1962

Of this quartet, the composer writes:

> [It] consists of many brief, contrasting connected movements. Often the ending phrase of one movement serves as the inspiration of the next one in a "stream of consciousness" fashion. Towards the end there are some allusions to "Tristan" and Schubert, meant to be understood as tongue-in-cheek homage. [record jacket notes, by Alan Hershowitz, *String Quartets* Leonarda #111]

Beginning slowly, progressing from low to high register, the tempo changes frequently, as Schonthal utilizes special effects and special timbres. Throughout the entire work many melodies and/or melodic fragments dominate. The texture is, for the most part, more that of accompanied melody than of contrapuntal density.

The middle section is often reminiscent of early-twentieth-century Romantic wanderings within a vague key center. Schonthal makes abundant use of the first violin in spinning out her melodies, and the references to Wagner's *Tristan* occur here.

In the section that follows immediately, Schonthal makes use of Spanish dance rhythms, with the melody in the first violin and the rhythmic accompaniment in the other strings. Ending on a tonal open fifth cadence on *D*, this rhythmic section leads to the final one, which is somewhat similar to the beginning. The cello here assumes a lyrical solo.

References to Schubert occur in dotted rhythms just before the final ending, again on a tonal open fifth cadence on *D*.

List of Works
Vocal

The Courtship of Camilla, one-act opera (1979–80, Oxford University Press)
By the Roadside, for soprano (1975), on a text by Walt Whitman

3 canciones (3 songs) for soprano, flute, viola, cello, and harp (1956), on a text by Federico García Lorca

9 lyric-dramatic songs for mezzo-soprano (1960), on a text by William Butler Yeats

The Solitary Reaper, for tenor, flute, violin, cello, and piano (1978), on a text by William Wordsworth

7 songs of love and sorrow, for soprano (1977)

3 songs with words by Li Po, for soprano (1942)

Songs with words by R. M. Rilke, for soprano (1939–42)

Totengesänge ("Songs of Death"), for soprano (1963), text by composer

Operatic Cradle Song, for soprano, alto, and piano (1987)

Six Times Solitude, for soprano and piano, on a text by A. A. Milne (1986)

Piano

Canticles of Hieronymus (1987)

Capriccio español ("Spanish caprice") (1945)

Bird calls (1945; Oxford)

From North and South of the Border (Youngstown Press)

Miniatures, vols. 1, 2, and 3 (Galaxy Music)

Miniscules (Fischer)

Near and Far (Fischer)

Potpourrie (Fischer)

3 *Elegies for a Murder Victim* (1982)

Fiestas y danzas (1961)

Fragments from a Woman's Diary (1982)

12 *Inventions a due voci* (1984)

Nachklänge ("Reverberations"), for piano, with added timbres (1967–74)

Gestures, 11 pieces (1978)

Sonata brève (1973; Oxford)

Sonata quasi un'improvisazione (1964)

Sonatensatz ("Sonata movement") (1973)

Sonatina in A (1939, Lundgren [Stockholm])

Variations in Search of a Theme (Oxford)

Chamber

4 epiphanies for solo viola (1975; Oxford)

Fantasia in a Nostalgic Mood for Guitar (1978)

Interlude for solo harp (1980; Sisra Press)

14 *Inventions a due voci,* for harpsichord

Love Letters, for clarinet and cello (Sisra)

Music for Horn and Piano (1978)
String Quartet 1 (1962)
String Quartet 2 (1983)
Sonata for Violin and Piano in E (1962)
Sonata concertante for cello and piano (1973)
Sonata for cello (1988)

Orchestral

Candide Suite for Orchestra (1955)
The Transposed Heads, suite for orchestra (1963)
Concerto romantico (1942)
Concerto No. 2 (1977)
Music for Horn and Chamber Orchestra (1978)
6 Preludes (1946)
Serenade for Strings (1962)
Symphony in B (1957)
Sinfonia brève (1986)

Chorus and Orchestra

The Young Dead Soldiers (1985)

Film Scores

Lantern Love

Discography

4 Epiphanies: Orion ORS 83444
Fragments from a Woman's Diary: Orion ORS 85490
In Homage Of . . . (24 preludes): Orion ORS 85490
Loveletters: Capriccio CR 1001
Nachklänge ("Reverberations"): Orion ORS 81413
Quartet 1, for strings: Leonarda #111
Sonta brève: Orion ORS 81413
Sonata concertante: Orion ORS 83444
Sonata concertante, for clarinet and piano: Opus One
Sonatensatz ("Sonata movement"): Orion ORS 81413
Totengesänge (8 songs): Leonarda # 106
The Transposed Heads, ballet suite for orchestra: Columbia Records
Variations in Search of a Theme: Orion ORS 81413

Selected Bibliography

Brand, Helmig, Kaiser, Solomon, and Westerkamp. *Komponistinnen in Berlin* (a biography of Schonthal). Berlin: Hochschule der Kunst.

LePage, Jane Weiner. "Ruth Schonthal." In *Women Composers, Conductors and Musicians of the Twentieth Century,* vol. 3. Metuchen, NJ: Scarecrow Press, 1988.

Schonthal, Ruth *On Teaching Music Composition.* Forthcoming.

Sonntag and Matthei, eds. *Annäherungen* (Close-ups). Kassel, West Germany: Futura Verlag.

Zaimont, Judith, and Karen Famera, eds. *Contemporary Concert Music by Women.* Westport, CT: Greenwood Press, 1981. S. v. "Ruth Schonthal."

To contact the composer, write to:
The American Music Center
250 West 54th St. (Rm. 300)
New York, NY 10019

Barbara Kolb

(b. 1939)

New Vistas

Biographical Summary

1939	Born in Hartford, Connecticut, February 10.
1957	Begins undergraduate studies at the Hartt School of Music of the University of Hartford, in Connecticut.
1961–64	Teaches clarinet and music theory at Hartt School while studying composition with Arnold Franchetti. Plays clarinet in Hartford Symphony Orchestra.
1961	Receives Bachelor of Music, cum laude, from Hartt School of Music.
1964	Receives fellowship to study composition with Gunther Schuller and Lukas Foss at the Berkshire Music Festival, Tanglewood, Lenox, Massachusetts
1965	Receives Master of Music degree in composition from Hartt School. Moves to New York City.
1966	Receives Fulbright Grant to study in Vienna.
1968	Returns to Tanglewood to study with Gunther Schuller. Receives first of several fellowships to compose at the MacDowell Colony, Peterbor-

	ough, New Hampshire (returning there in 1969, 1971, 1972, 1980, 1983, 1987, and 1988).
1969	Receives the Prix de Rome in composition, the first time this prestigious award is given to a U.S. woman.
1969–71	Lives in Rome.
1971	Composes *Solitaire,* the first in a series of five works utilizing prerecorded tape.
1972	Named a trustee of the American Academy in Rome.
1973	Composer-in-residence at the Marlboro Music Festival, Vermont.
1973–75	Assistant Professor of Music Theory at Brooklyn College, New York
1975	Performance of orchestral version of *Soundings* by the New York Philharmonic, conducted by Pierre Boulez and David Gilbert.
1976–77	Works independently in Paris, having received a second Guggenheim Fellowship.
1978	Visiting professor of composition at Temple University, Philadelphia.
	Performance of *Soundings* by Seiji Ozawa, Symphony Hall, Boston, then taken on tour to Japan.
1979	Premiere of first orchestral work, *Grisaille,* Portland Symphony Orchestra, Oregon.
1979–81	Appointed Artistic Director of Contemporary Music at the Third Street Music Settlement School, New York City. Founds and directs "Music New to New York," a concert series of new contemporary music.
1981	Works in Italy on the film *Cantico,* on the life of St. Francis of Assisi.
1982	Begins work on a music theory course for the blind and physically handicapped, sponsored by the Library of Congress.
1983–84	Works on computer-generated music at the Institut de Recherche et de Co-ordination Acoustique/ Musique (IRCAM), Paris.
1984–85	Visiting Professor of Composition at the Eastman School of Music, Rochester, New York.
1985	Performance of *Grisaille,* Pittsburgh Symphony Orchestra.

	Premiere of *Millefoglie,* a piece for computer-generated tape and chamber ensemble, Paris.
1986	Completes coursework for the blind and physically handicapped, available on cassette tape from Library of Congress.
	Commission and performance of *Umbrian Colors,* for violin and guitar, Marlboro Music Festival, Vermont.
1987	*Yet That Things Go Round,* for chamber orchestra, commissioned by the Fromm Foundation and premiered by the New York Chamber Symphony in May.
	Awarded second prize ($2500) in the prestigious Friedheim Competition at the Kennedy Center, Washington, D.C., for *Millefoglie.* Her former teacher Gunther Schuller won first prize.
1988	Performance of *Yet That Things Go Round,* Aspen Summer Music Festival; performance of *Millefoglie,* Dallas Symphony Orchestra.
	Lives in New York City.

The first U.S. woman to receive the prestigious Prix de Rome in composition (1969), and the second-prize winner in the 1987 Friedheim Competition, Barbara Kolb has also been the recipient of many awards, including three Tanglewood Fellowships, four MacDowell Fellowships, and two Guggenheim Fellowships. Among the many grants she has received are those from the Institute of Arts and Letters and the National Endowment for the Arts. Her works have been performed by such world-class ensembles as the New York Philharmonic, the Boston Symphony Orchestra, and the Pittsburgh Symphony.

Primarily an instrumental composer, she has also incorporated aspects of electronic music in her works, especially prerecorded performances on tape, which are an integral part of several of her compositions. Her work with electronic tape has expanded to include the background music, a tape collage, for the film *Cantico* (1982), based on the life of St. Francis of Assisi.

An accomplished clarinetist, Kolb began serious study of composition while a college student at the Hartt School of Music. Awarded her first fellowship to Tanglewood in 1964, she had the privilege of studying with the well-known U.S. composers Gunther Schuller and Lukas Foss.

Kolb's music is representative of several recent trends. Among these are a special interest in the music of other cultures, which in Kolb's case are mainly Japanese, Italian, and French; a special sensitivity to other arts, namely, the visual arts and poetry; and the combining of prerecorded sound with live performances.

When asked to describe Kolb's music, the Japanese composer Toru Takemitsu commented: "It is always my great pleasure to listen to Barbara's music, which is filled with affluent imagination" (as quoted in a Boosey and Hawkes promotional brochure).

Much of her music seeks to create an atmosphere, and with little or no reference to established forms or systems. Perhaps her musical imagination is best exemplified by her feeling for tone color and her unusual combinations of instruments. Her *Chromatic Fantasy* (1979), for instance, calls for narrator, amplified alto flute, oboe, soprano saxophone, trumpet, and amplified electric guitar and vibraphone. Her *Trobar Clus* (1970), dedicated to her teacher Lukas Foss, calls for a chamber ensemble of three wind instruments, a percussion battery of bells, vibraphone, marimba, cymbals, maracas, and wind chimes, an amplified harpsichord, guitar, and three strings.

Kolb is the daughter of a self-taught musician, Harold Judson Kolb, an organist, pianist, and composer of popular music, who was the director of music for WTIC radio station in Hartford, Connecticut, and the conductor of many semiprofessional big bands of his time. His influence was considerable during her early musical training, as Kolb states: "I often sang on the radio when I was little. . . . When you're an only child and your father is music director, you get these opportunities. . . . Once I even made some records of old songs—things like 'Paper Doll' " (*The Hartford Courant*, April 7, 1987).

During the early 1960s, Kolb played clarinet in the Hartford Summer Band and the Hartford Symphony Orchestra. Commenting on her six-year stint as an orchestral player, Kolb asserts: "Orchestra work did not provide for individual creativity, due to the fact that playing continually in an orchestra provides no stimulation and is basically a boring mini-intellectual experience, allowing no room for growth" (LePage, 117).

Upon graduation from college, Kolb moved to New York City and supplemented her income by working as a music copyist. In 1973 she received her first full-time teaching appointment, as a professor of composition and musical analysis at Brooklyn College.

Although Kolb has never accepted a long-term teaching post, she has encouraged other young composers by programming their works on her concert series, "Music New to New York." She has supported herself with short-term teaching assignments, but at present, like Ellen Zwilich, Kolb devotes herself first and foremost to composing; her current situation is made possible by continued performances, commissions, awards, and grants. Kolb is fortunate in having an exclusive contract with the

Six Living U.S. Composers

music publisher Boosey and Hawkes, a company that has entered into contracts with such twentieth-century giants as Igor Stravinsky, Béla Bartók, Aaron Copland, and Benjamin Britten. Kolb speaks about the incentive that such a contract provides:

> A tremendous revelation occurs when you realize that a company of the stature of Boosey and Hawkes is truly interested in you and will publish everything you write. . . . There is a whole new attitude that develops when you discover that people actually like your music. Writing music is a very painful process and it is very solitary. With the recognition from Boosey and Hawkes, there is a feeling of responsibility to them, not just to myself, which is a tremendous incentive to continue. [LePage, 119]

In spite of her success as a composer, Kolb feels that women still have a long way to go in being recognized in the male-dominated field of music composition:

> People say, "Oh, how wonderful you've made it in this profession," but I'm not so sure I have. As a woman composer, I am in some ways a novelty, since there are very few of us who have had international exposure. So, yes, in that respect it's true. But in comparison to some of my male colleagues who are roughly my age—people like Joe Schwanter, David Del Tredici, John Harbison—I'm not doing so well, really . . . I mean, I don't even have a job. I don't think I want to dwell on what it means specifically to be a woman in the composing field . . . although I will say this: when you're young, when you're up and coming, nobody cares much whether you're a woman. When you get older and the money gets bigger, it's a little different. To be a peer is not necessarily what a lot of men composers want you to be. Recognition is fine, but I'm at a point in my life where remuneration means something. [*Hartford Courant*, April 7, 1987]

Kolb's future directions in musical composition might lead elsewhere. She admits a fascination with writing film scores, an area in which women composers have received little encouragement. "Someday I would like to write background music for film because I like film people for one thing and I like theater for another and I like drama in general. It also pays money" (LePage, 131).

Kolb may be one of the first women composers who will be able to make a significant contribution to the film industry. The success of her film score, *Cantico*, indicates that we may be able to see "Music composed by Barbara Kolb" on more films' lists of credits.

Musical Example
Homage to Keith Jarrett and Gary Burton
1976

Describing how this work came into being, the composer explains her first excursion into jazz:

> [In 1976] I had become extremely interested in the music of Keith Jarrett, and wanted to express myself in a similar style, in spite of the fact that I had never had any direct experience in jazz improvisation. . . . My entire musical education had been influenced by the "masters," and I felt a need to be uninhibited and free from this disciplined background.

Regarding the genesis of the musical material that served as a starting point for Kolb's quasi-improvisation, the composer explains:

> [It] is based on a 30-second improvisation of a tune entitled "Grow Your Own" (an early song of Jarrett's) which I literally stole from the record. Having this skeletal outline, I then worked my material around that of Jarrett's, creating a potpourri of Jarrett, Kolb, and reminiscences of my past. [Kolb, *Homage to Keith Jarrett and Gary Burton* (New York: Boosey and Hawkes, 1976), as quoted in the jacket notes, *New Music for the Flute* Leonarda #121]

The atmosphere of this work is not "jazzy," and yet it does represent an improvisational technique in its own way. The melodic lines of the flute are often spun out at great length, punctuated by vibraphone chords or improvisations that often produce a separate melodic line of their own. This ten-minute work is reflective more than virtuosic, more concerned with sound representation than with technical brilliance.

Selected List of Works
Orchestral

Grisaille (1978–79, Boosey and Hawkes)
Soundings, for 2 conductors and orchestra (1971–72; revised 1975 and 1978; Boosey and Hawkes)
Yet That Things Go Round (1986–87; Boosey and Hawkes)

Ensemble

Chromatic Fantasy, for narrator and chamber ensemble (1979; Boosey and Hawkes)
Crosswinds, for wind ensemble and percussion (1968; Boosey and Hawkes)

Millefoglie, for computer tape and chamber orchestra (1984–85; Boosey and Hawkes)

The Point That Divides the Wind, for organ, 4 percussionists, and 3 male voices (1982; Boosey and Hawkes).

Trobar Clus, for chamber ensemble (1970; Boosey and Hawkes)

Solo Tape

Cantico, tape collage score for the film on the life of St. Francis of Assisi (1982)

Instrumental and Chamber Works with or without Voice

Appello, for piano (1976; Boosey and Hawkes)

Cavatina, for solo violin or viola (1983)

Chansons bas, for lyric soprano, harp, and 2 percussionists (1966; Fischer)

Figments, for flute and piano (1967; revised 1969; Fischer)

Homage to Keith Jarrett and Gary Burton, for flute and vibraphone (1976; Boosey and Hawkes)

Looking for Claudio, for guitar and prerecorded tape (1975; Boosey and Hawkes)

Rebuttal, for 2 clarinets (1965; C. F. Peters)

Related Characters, for trumpet (or clarinet, alto sax, viola and piano) (1980)

Solitaire, for piano and prerecorded tape (1971; Peters)

Songs Before an Adieu, for soprano, flute, and guitar (1976–79; Boosey and Hawkes)

Spring River Flowers Moon Night, for 2 pianos and prerecorded tape (1974–75; Boosey and Hawkes)

Three Lullabies, for guitar (1980; Boosey and Hawkes)

Three Place Settings, for narrator, clarinet, violin, double bass, and percussion (1968; Fischer)

Toccata, for harpsichord and prerecorded tape (1971; Peters)

Umbrian Colors, for guitar and violin (1986; Boosey and Hawkes)

Discography

Chansons bas: Desto DC-7143

Crosswinds: Galaxia Gal. 004

Figments: Desto DC-7143

Homage to Keith Jarrett and Gary Burton: Leonarda #121

Looking for Claudio: Composers Recordings, Inc. CRI-SD-361

Rebuttal: Opus One #14

The Sentences (from *Songs Before an Adieu*): Turnabout TV-S 34727

Solitaire: Turnabout TV-34487

Songs Before an Adieu: Bridge BDG-2004

Spring River Flowers Moon Night: Composers Recordings, Inc. CRI-SD 361

Three Lullabies: Bridge BDG-2001

Selected Bibliography

Kimmelman, Michael. "Music: Kolb Premiere, by Chamber Symphony." *The New York Times,* May 4, 1987.

LePage, Jane Weiner. "Barbara Kolb." In *Women Composers, Conductors, and Musicians of the Twentieth Century,* vol. 1. Metuchen, NJ: The Scarecrow Press, 1980.

Metcalf, Steve. "Coming Home Sounds Sweet to Composer." *The Hartford Courant,* April 7, 1987.

The New Grove Dictionary of American Music. H. Wiley Hitchcock and Stanley Sadie, eds. London and New York: Macmillan Press Ltd, 1986. S.v. 'Kolb, Barbara," by Lawrence Starr.

Perlmutter, Donna. "The Composer in a Gender Ghetto?" *The Los Angeles Times,* April 6, 1986.

For more information or to contact Barbara Kolb, write to her publisher and agent:

Boosey and Hawkes Publishers
24 W. 57th St.
New York, NY 10019
212-757-3332

or contact:

The American Music Center
250 W. 54th St. (Rm. 300)
New York, NY 10019

Marga Richter

(b. 1926)

Chamber Music and Orchestral Composer

Biographical Summary

1926	Born in Reedsburg, Wisconsin, on October 21 into a musical family.
1929	Begins to study piano in Minneapolis; composed small pieces as a child.
1945	Begins study at the Juilliard School of Music, New York City.
1949	Receives Bachelor of Music from the Juilliard School, majoring in composition. Studies piano with Rosalyn Tureck, and composition with Vincent Persichetti and William Bergsma.
1951	Receives Master's degree from the Juilliard School. Continues studies with Persichetti and Bergsma.
1953	Marries Alan Skelly, who would later become chairman of the Philosophy Department at C. W. Post College, Long Island.
1956	Birth of son, Michael.
1958	Birth of daughter, Maureen.
1956–71	Home-based, caring for her two children and composing in her spare time.

1971–73	Teaches at Nassau Community College, Long Island.
1972	Founds, with Herbert Dentich, the Long Island Composers' Alliance.
1975	Signs exclusive publishing contract with Carl Fischer, Inc.
1976	Performs her First Piano Concerto with Oklahoma Symphony.
1977–present	Composes and teaches at home on Long Island; performs many of her piano works in the United States and Europe; supervises new recordings of her works.

The music of Marga Richter came to national attention in the late 1950s as a result of a series of recordings by the MGM Record Company of her *Concerto for Piano and Violas, Cellos and Basses, Lament* for string orchestra, *Aria and Toccata for Viola and String Orchestra, Transmutation* for voice and piano, and *Two Chinese Songs,* also for voice and piano. These recordings featured major performers and conductors, among them pianists Ménahem Pressler and William Masselos, conductors Carlos Surinach and Izler Solomon, and violist Walter Trampler. Such recognition is highly unusual for a woman of such a young age; that this took place thirty years ago is especially remarkable.

While she was a student at the Juilliard School, studying piano with Rosalyn Tureck and composition with William Bergsma and Vincent Persichetti, several of Richter's compositions were performed at a Composers' Forum in New York City, receiving favorable reviews from both *The New York Times* and the *Herald Tribune.* Thus, in her early twenties, with this kind of recognition in the form of performances and reviews, Richter was encouraged to push forward toward new forms of musical expression.

Actually, Richter had always been encouraged to make music the focal point of her life. Her mother, Inez Chandler, was a noted singer, and her grandfather was the German composer-conductor Richard Richter. Her own musical gifts were early recognized and were fostered through piano and music theory lessons beginning at age five. Her family was so supportive of her talents that when Richter was accepted as a piano and composition student at Juilliard, her entire family moved from Wisconsin to New York City.

Throughout her composing career, Richter has written in a wide variety of genres: music for full orchestra, two concerti, music for string orchestra, piano solos, harpsichord pieces, music for strings, music for woodwinds, two pieces for brass, a large variety of vocal music, and several ballet scores.

It is almost impossible to categorize or generalize about the musical style of such a versatile composer. As is the case with much twentieth-century music, most commentaries about Richter's works come from concert reviews. Regarding her *Landscapes of the Mind I*, a piano concerto, critic R. L. Cherry wrote:

> This concerto, a well-crafted blend of realism and transcendentalism, and of the East and West, is unconventional but not eccentric, occasionally dissonant, but not offensive, individual and original but not avant-garde. It is a complex but uncomplicated psychomusical experience. [*Musical America*, 1976]

Of her *Sonata for Piano*, critic Celliot Zucherman observed:

> Marga Richter's Sonata is rich and powerful. Its large proportions and full use of every sort of piano technique place it, as she intended, in the tradition of the big sonatas of the nineteenth century. [*American Record Guide*, 1956]

And regarding the musical example discussed here, *Landscapes of the Mind II*, Alan Hughes commented:

> Miss Richter's piece . . . is written in such a way that it responded to Mr. Heifetz's way of playing, and it made a favorable impression on this listener . . . the contrasts of energy and mood are handled adroitly, and hold the interest for the twelve minutes or so that the work lasts. [*New York Times*, 1977]

Commentary from the composer reveals a free spirit, uninhibited by her intense musical training:

> I've never followed any prescribed theory or system of composition. I think of my music as intensely personal, fitting no prescribed mold, following no path but its own, belonging to no school or movement . . . and yet I see it belonging to the musical mainstream. [Promotional brochure from Magna Carta Management]

Her own way of composing, she admits, is "painfully slow"; she sometimes spends twelve or more hours on a single measure. She never erases, but simply throws earlier efforts on the floor. She is then able to retrieve discarded sketches, should they prove to be better than the later ones.

The composer, whose inspiration often comes from nonmusical sources, such as the Georgia O'Keeffe paintings that inspired *Landscapes of the Mind,* sums up her own artistic credo:

> Just as [Georgia O'Keeffe] didn't believe in theories, but rather just tried to fill the space of her canvases in a beautiful way . . . I just try to make my music as beautiful as I can, and hope others will find it beautiful too. [Magna Carta Management]

A distinguished pianist, Richter has not only performed many of her piano works; she has also composed several pedagogical pieces for young students. Among these works, which she refers to as "educational pieces," are: "A Farewell" (1961), "Four Piano Pieces" (1971), "The Lost People" (1965), and "Two Short Suites for Young Pianists" (1947).

Since the late 1960s, Richter has been the recipient of many grants and awards, including ones from the National Endowment for the Arts, the Martha Baird Rockefeller Fund, and The National Federation of Music Clubs, as well as commissions from the Minnesota Orchestra, the Milwaukee Symphony, and the Buffalo Philharmonic. The Joffrey, the Harkness, and the Boston ballet companies have danced her ballet *Abyss* (1964). The majority of Richter's compositions have been published, and her music is well represented on commercial recordings, an impressive accomplishment for any twentieth-century composer.

Marga Richter has devoted considerable thought and energy to the cause of women in music. She was one of the founders of the League of Women Composers, and as a member of its Board of Directors, she helped organize many concerts of women composers. Furthermore, she has articulated her views on the question of a feminine aesthetic in music:

> In private, the men mostly seem to feel that women's music is weaker. . . . For a long time I believed that myself. Many of the reviews of my music said things like . . . "It would seem impossible that this pungent and virile composition could be the creation of a woman." . . .

> Today I feel quite differently. Not long ago Karel Husa, a Pulitzer Prize winning composer, wrote me, "All your works have the same qualities: gentleness, deep feeling, long phrasing, contrapuntally clear lines, all very sensitive qualities we do not hear too often, perhaps because they are feminine." I take Mr. Husa's statement as a very real compliment, for I think he may have hit upon something. When we have enough music by women to make a study of the question, we may find that women are able to express emotion in a different way. . . . I don't think men can write music like women . . . nor vice versa. After all, I am a woman, and I express what I am. [LePage, vol. 1, pp. 222–23]

One must applaud Richter for expressing her ideas on this subject, as they are controversial among women composers at the present time. As for the years she spent raising a family, Richter maintains that she never regarded her role as wife and mother as a burden: "I'm glad . . . that I didn't have commissions coming in and deadlines to meet while the kids were growing up. To tell them to go away, I'm busy—I don't think I could have done this. Your kids are only home once, even if you live to be a hundred" (LePage, p. 214). Both of her children have inherited some of their mother's musical talent. Her daughter has studied sitar in India, and her son, a professional pianist, is featured on the musical example presented here.

Musical Example
Landscapes of the Mind II
for violin and piano, middle section
1971

One of three *Landscapes of the Mind,* all of which were inspired by two paintings by Georgia O'Keeffe ("Sky Clouds II" and "Pelvis I"), this second landscape is scored for solo violin and piano. The first landscape, scored as a concerto for piano and orchestra, was actually written after the second, in 1974, and the last landscape, scored as a piano trio, was composed in 1978. About this trilogy composed over a period of seven years, Richter reflects:

> The pieces seek to convey the spaciousness and serenity of the O'Keeffe paintings, contrasted with inner turbulence, urgency, and ultimate isolation. In addition to sharing thematic material, each piece also has music unique to itself. All are essentially one-movement works, in many contrasting sections which paradoxically are closely inter-related, giving an overall impression of freedom and fantasy in construction and effect. [Jacket notes, *Clarinet, Violin, Piano,* Leonarda #122]

The middle section, recorded here, is preceded by a quiet and slow introduction of solo piano, followed by a short commentary by the violin. Very often the piano part is a simple ostinato, but after the opening section, both violin and piano become more intense. The tempo quickens and the texture becomes more complex.

This middle section contains brief references to a waltz. The return to the quiet atmosphere of the first section finds the violin playing an extended lyrical melody, accompanied by just two alternating chords in the piano.

The final section begins with the piano repeating a slow version of the waltz theme, punctuated by short comments from the violin. The piece concludes with a frenzied display of fluctuating tempi in both violin and piano, followed by a final subdued reference to the opening section.

This piece was composed for violinist Daniel Heifetz, who performed it in the International Tchaikovsky Competition in Moscow.

Selected List of Works
Orchestra

Landscapes of the Mind I (Concerto No. 2 for piano and orchestra) (1974; Fischer)
Aria and Toccata, for viola and string orchestra (1957; Belwin Mills)
Lament, string orchestra (1956; Broude Brothers)
Concerto for piano, violas, cellos, and double bass (1955; Fischer)
Blackberry Vines and Winter Fruit (1976; Fischer)
8 pieces for orchestra or piano (1961; Fischer)
Fragments (1976; Fischer)
Variations on a Sarabande (1959; Fischer)
Music for 3 quintets and orchestra (wind, brass, and string quintets) (1978; Fischer)
Out of Shadows and Solitude (1986; Fischer)
Düsseldorf Concerto (1982; Fischer)

Brass

One for Two and Two for Three (trombone duets and trios) (1947; 1974; Fischer)
Ricercare, for brass quartet (1958; Fischer)
Obsessions, for solo trombone (1986)

Band

Country Auction (1976; Fischer)

Chamber

String Quartet No. 2 (1975; Fischer)
Landscapes of the Mind III, for violin, cello, and piano (1976; Fischer)
Sonata for clarinet and piano (1948; Fischer)
Pastorale, for 2 oboes (1975; Fischer)
Landscapes of the Mind II, for violin and piano (1971; Fischer)
Suite for violin and piano (1975; Fischer)

Sonata for 2 clarinets and piano (1975; Fischer)
Suite for viola (1961)
Sonora, for two clarinets and piano (1981; Presser)
Exequy, for oboe, clarinet, cello, and piano (1983)
Seacliff Variations (1984)
Qhanri (Snow Mountain), Tibetan variations for cello and piano (1986)

Organ

Variations on a Theme by Neidhart von Reuenthal (1974; Fischer)

Piano

Variations on a Theme by Latimer (1964; Fischer)
Bird of Yearning (1976; Fischer)
Melodrama for 2 pianos (1958; Fischer)
4 piano pieces, educational
Requiem (1978; Elkan-Vogel)
Fragments (1963; Fischer)
Remembrances (1971; Elkan-Vogel)
Piano Sonata (1954; Fischer)
2 short suites for young pianists (educational piece) (1947)
8 pieces for piano (1961; Fischer)
Exequy (1980; Presser)

Vocal

She at His Funeral, for voice and piano, on a text by Thomas Hardy
   (1954; Fischer)
3 songs of madness and death, for mixed chorus (Fischer)
Transmutation, a song cycle for voice and piano (1949; Fischer)
2 Chinese songs, for voice and piano (1953; Fischer)
8 songs to Chinese texts
To whom?, based on a text by Virginia Woolf, for soprano, alto, tenor,
   and bass, a cappella (1980; Presser)
Do not press my hands, on a text by G. Mistral, for two sopranos, alto,
   tenor, and bass (1981; Presser)
Später einmal, on a text by F. Tanzer, for solo voice and piano (1981;
   Presser)
Three songs on poems by Emily Dickinson, for two sopranos and two
   altos, a cappella (1982; Schirmer)
Lament for Art O'Leary, for soprano and piano (1984)
Sieben Lieder, for solo voice and piano (1985)

Sacred

Psalm 91, for mixed chorus, a cappella (1963; Elkan-Vogel)
Seek Him (Amos 5:8), for mixed chorus, a cappella (1965; Fischer)
3 Christmas songs for children's chorus and 2 flutes or piano (1964)

Ballet

Abyss (1964; Belwin Mills)
Bird of Yearning (1967; Fischer)
The Servant
4 unpublished ballet scores (1951–52)

Harpsichord

Short prelude in Baroque style (1974; Fischer)
Soundings (1965; Fischer)

Discography

Sonata for Piano: Metro-Goldwyn-Mayer E 3244
Concerto for Piano and Violas, Cellos, and Basses: MGM E 3547
Lament: MGM E 3422; Leonarda #327 (CD)
Aria and Toccata for Viola and Strings: MGM E 3559
Transmutation and *Two Chinese Songs:* MGM E 3546
Two Short Suites for Young Pianists: MGM E 3417
Landscapes of the Mind II: Leonarda #122
Sonora, for two clarinets and piano: Leonarda #122

Selected Bibliography

Hear and Now: An Explanation of the Creative Mind, Program 3. A Project of New York Women Composers with Judith St. Croix. American Cable Systems. 1988. Distributed by New York Women Composers, New York. Video tape.
Henry, Derrick. "Atlanta Symphony, Soloist Shine in Difficult Piano Concerto." *The Atlantic Constitution,* March 22, 1986.
LePage, Jane Weiner. "Marga Richter," In *Women Composers, Conductors, and Musicians of the Twentieth Century,* vol. 1. Metuchen, NJ, and London: The Scarecrow Press, 1980.
The New Grove Dictionary of American Music, ed. H. Wiley Hitchcock and Stanley Sadie. London and New York: Macmillan Press, 1986. S.v. "Richter, Marga" by Judith Rosen.

To contact Marga Richter, write to her Concert Manager:
Sylvia Craft
Magna Carta Management
101 Runnymeade Dr.
East Hampton, NY 11937

Judith Lang Zaimont

(b. 1945)

Pianist, Author, Composer

Biographical Summary

1945	Born in Memphis, Tennessee, into a musical family, on November 8.
Early Childhood	Studies piano with her mother. Begins composing at age 12.
1958–64	On a scholarship to the Juilliard Preparatory School, studies piano with Rosina Lhevinne and theory and duo-piano with Ann Hull.
1960–67	Performs with her sister, Doris Lang, in two-piano team, touring the United States, appearing on television shows, and making recordings.
1962	Wins Junior Composers' competitions, sponsored by The National Federation of Music Clubs. Performs her *Portrait of a City* (a piano suite) in Washington, D.C. Enters Queens College of the City University of New York.
1963	Decides to concentrate on composition.
1964	Wins the Broadcast Music, Inc., Student Composers' Award for her *Four Songs for Mezzo-Soprano and Piano*.
1965–66	Studies composition with Hugo Weisgall.

211

1966	Receives Bachelor's degree in music from Queens College.
	Studies composition with Jack Beeson; receives Broadcast Music, Inc. (B.M.I.) award.
	Receives an artist's diploma in piano from the Long Island Institute of Music.
1967	Marries Gary Zaimont, artist and teacher.
1967–68	Studies composition with Otto Leuning.
1968	Receives Master's degree in music composition from Columbia University.
1967–71	Accompanist and resident composer of the Great Neck Choral Society, New York.
1969–71	Lecturer in musicology at the New York City Community College.
1971	Receives first prize in the Gottschalk Competition and second prize in the Delius Composition contest.
	Wins a MacDowell Fellowship for study at the MacDowell Colony.
1971–72	On a Debussy Scholarship, studies orchestration in Paris at the Alliance Française with composer André Jolivet.
1972–74	Self-teaching of orchestration.
1972–76	Instructor at Queens College.
1976–78	Teaches privately (piano and composition) in Queens, New York.
1977	First recordings, on the Golden Crest label.
1980–86	Faculty member, Peabody Conservatory, Baltimore, Maryland.
1981	Birth of her son Michael.
1983–84	Wins a Guggenheim Fellowship, permitting her a year's leave of absence from teaching.
1984	Publication of *The Musical Woman*, vol. 1, by the Greenwood Press.
1985	Receives "Teacher of the Year" award from Peabody Conservatory.
1987	Publication of *The Musical Woman*, vol. 2, by the Greenwood Press.
	Awarded the 1987 Paul Revere Prize from the Music Publishers Association for her choral piece *The Chase*.
	Composer-in-residence, Wesleyan University, Middletown, Connecticut.

Premiere of *The Magic World*, song cycle for baritone, piano, and percussion, Festival Chamber Players, Long Island.

Premiere of *Fanfare '87*, for brass ensemble, commissioned by Queens College in celebration of its 50th anniversary.

Hidden Heritage (A Dance Symphony), a ballet score, performed by the Baltimore Dance Theater, Columbia, Maryland.

1988   February: *Wind Quintet*, commissioned by the Vox Nova Quintet, premieres at Weill Recital Hall, Carnegie Hall.

April: Premiere of *Monarchs*, a full orchestral work, Greenville Symphony, Greenville, South Carolina, Victoria Bond, conductor.

May: Premiere of *Sacred Service*, Princeton Pro Musica chorus and orchestra, David Arnold, solo, Princeton, New Jersey.

Awarded scholarship in music composition by the National League of American Pen Women.

Lives and works on Long Island, New York.

In addition to being the composer of over seventy art songs, several orchestral works, an opera, a wide variety of instrumental and vocal chamber works, numerous works for chorus, and many piano works, Judith Zaimont has also established herself as an editor-author, a concertizing and recorded pianist, and an outstanding teacher who, in 1985, was recognized as teacher of the year by the Peabody Conservatory in Baltimore.

For a woman of her age, her catalogue of works and her musical accomplishments are impressive. The many prizes, awards, and commissions she has received include: ten ASCAP awards, ten prizes from the National Federation of Music Clubs, two Delius composition prizes, The Presser Foundation Award, a Guggenheim Fellowship, a Woodrow Wilson Fellowship, and the Debussy Fellowship for study in France.

Her works have been commissioned and programmed by major performing groups in this country, including the Gregg Smith Singers, the Primavera String Quartet, the Connecticut Opera, the Florilegium Chamber Choir, and the Baltimore Symphony. Much of her music has been published and recorded, and performances are now proliferating for this gifted and versatile young composer.

But she has not always been a composer. Like most of her predecessors, she was first a performer, and like most of the other living U.S.

women discussed in this section, she comes from a musical family. Her mother is a music teacher who, while her children were growing up, occasionally composed popular songs and wrote entire musical shows for the schools where she taught. Zaimont and her sister, the conductor Doris Lang Kosloff, studied piano with their mother until they entered the Juilliard Preparatory School. One of their piano teachers was Ann Hull, who had been the keyboard partner of composer Mary Howe (1882–1964); naturally, the Lang sisters played some of Mary Howe's music.

During their teenage years, the Lang sisters received national recognition, appearing as individual soloists on several Lawrence Welk shows, and later, as a team, on three Mitch Miller television programs, in addition to touring the country. During this time, the sisters made a professional recording, *Concert for Two Pianos* (Golden Crest CR 4070), and also made their debut with the Little Orchestra Society in Carnegie Hall, in 1963. They continued their professional appearances until 1967 when both entered graduate school.

Zaimont's principal teacher of composition at Queens College was Hugo Weisgall, but she also studied privately with Leo Kraft, in order to learn twentieth-century composition techniques. In graduate school at Columbia University, Zaimont studied with Jack Beeson and Otto Leuning. Considering the influence these teachers may have exerted, Zaimont reflects: "Weisgall and Beeson may have influenced me, since I write a tremendous amount of music for voice, and they both are heavily concentrated in vocal music. Leuning gave me a wonderful sense of anything goes—one need not wear a stylistic strait-jacket" (LePage, p. 325).

Of André Jolivet, with whom she studied in Paris from 1971–1972, Zaimont recalls: "Jolivet received me as a colleague rather than a student—an exhilarating change in status" (LePage, p. 326). With Jolivet she studied orchestration, and composed, among other things, a *Concerto for Piano and Orchestra*.

In the early 1970s, Zaimont started to receive commissions to compose. Among her more important works of that period are: *Chansons Nobles et Sentimentales* (five songs for high voice and piano on texts by Charles Baudelaire, Paul Verlaine, and Arthur Rimbaud), commissioned by Michael Trimble of the Cleveland Institute of Music; *Songs of Innocence* (four songs on texts by William Blake, for soprano and tenor voices, flute, cello, and harp), commissioned by Gregg Smith; and *Sunny Airs and Sober* (five madrigals for chorus, a cappella), commissioned by the Waldorf Singers. Conductor Gregg Smith, of the Gregg Smith Singers, who has recorded and performed several of Zaimont's choral works, has commented:

I consider Judith Zaimont to be a woman of extraordinary talent as a composer and pianist, and one of the most musical individuals I have known. She writes music that has a great deal of expressive strength and rhythmic vitality. In the field of choral music, she has written several excellent works that, in addition to the above qualities, also show a true innate skill in vocal writing. [LePage, p. 327]

Zaimont is known primarily as a composer of solo and chamber vocal music, although she has composed in a variety of other genres. In 1975, following the premiere of her *Greyed Sonnets,* for soprano and piano, Raymond Ericson of *The New York Times* wrote:

The evening also offered Judith Lang Zaimont's *Greyed Sonnets,* a fine setting of five poems by Edna St. Vincent Millay, Sara Teasdale, and Christina Rossetti. The music is strongly emotional, suiting the texts, yet carefully constructed. [*New York Times,* November 20, 1975]

Zaimont herself has often articulated how she searches for a text, and eventually sets it to music:

I'm very particular about what texts I set: I'll go to the library and take out an entire shelf of poetry anthologies just to find three or four individual poems suitable for use as lyrics. . . . I chose the poems of *Greyed Sonnets* after being introduced to the writings of Edna St. Vincent Millay. As a modern romantic, I felt akin to many of her sentiments. . . . Very often I will hear in my head a linear contour, a rhythmic setting—in short, the whole musical setting, complete. I try to develop vocal lines independent of the instrumental parts. [LePage, pp. 328 and 329]

Perhaps one of her most dramatic vocal chamber works is *The Magic World: Ritual Music for Three* (1979–80), scored for bass baritone, various percussion instruments, and piano. Based on excerpts from American Indian poems and chants, the twenty-minute song cycle uses a wide variety of instrumental color, including the glockenspiel, finger cymbals, piano strings, wood blocks, cow bells, claves, tubular bells, and tom-toms. The middle song, ''The Whirlwind,'' is especially representative of Zaimont's dramatic style.

Also of special interest is her vocal-chamber composition *From the Great Land: Women's Songs* (1982). Commissioned by the North Star Consort of the University of Alaska, the work is based on Eskimo songs: ''She Is Left on the Ice,'' ''Passion: The First Dream,'' ''Lullaby: The Second Dream,'' ''Counting Song: The Third Dream,'' ''Lament—Interlude—Lullaby,'' ''Vision,'' and ''She Dies.'' A large and dramatic work, *From the Great Land* is scored for mezzo-soprano, clarinet, piano, and Eskimo drum. Its first performance took place in Bayreuth, Germany, in May 1982.

Zaimont's most recent commissions have been for orchestral works. Taking a cue from the recent review of *Monarchs,* one eagerly awaits the creation of a Symphony No. 1 by Judith Zaimont:

> This single movement piece is a work that utilizes with persuasive eloquence a wide range of orchestral colors and compositional techniques. Zaimont lays out in clear display her formal concepts, contained masterfully by a centrifugal moving tonality that never lacks direction. Though at times riding a nebulous lyricism, the music is primarily straightforward and dramatic. [*The Greenville Times* (South Carolina) April 24, 1988]

Judith Lang Zaimont is becoming recognized as one of the major talents among America's young composers. As the number of commissions and performances of her works increases, Zaimont has decided, at this writing, to devote herself full-time to composing.

Dedicated to furthering the cause of women in music, Zaimont is the editor of three major publications: *The Musical Woman,* volumes 1 and 2 (Greenwood Press, 1984 and 1987) and *Contemporary Concert Music of Women Composers* (Greenwood Press, 1981). She has been active in the League of Women Composers, as well as serving as composer-in-residence at national meetings on women in music.

She has also made a considerable contribution to piano pedagogy, as it relates to the teaching of twentieth-century performance techniques. Her "Annotated List of Twentieth Century Repertoire for the Piano" is now a standard teaching source, as published in *The Piano Teacher's Guidebook* (Yorktown Music Press, 1979).

As a composer, writer about music, and teacher, Judith Lang Zaimont has exhibited a formidable amount of musical and intellectual creativity in her young life. Her music continues to speak to an ever-widening audience. A first-class craftswoman and an inspired melodist, with a natural flare for dramatic and emotional impact, Judith Lang Zaimont is a major contributor to twentieth-century American music.

Musical Example
Nocturne: La Fin de Siècle
1978

This lyrical piece for solo piano sounds as though it were written in homage to the French composers of piano music who were active at the turn of the century, namely, Debussy, Ravel, and Fauré. However, in

Six Living U.S. Composers

speaking of her *Nocturne,* Zaimont enlarges upon the source of inspiration: "This piece is my personal 'valentine' to the great composer-pianists of the high Romantic age" (Jacket notes, *Judith Lang Zaimont,* Leonarda #101).

Cast in three sections, the first part opens in a slow and tentative minor tonality. The effect is almost improvisatory, but with a distinct melody spun out above a constantly moving eighth-note harmonic bass. The middle section is in sharp contrast to the two outer sections, not only in its faster tempo, *quasi doppio movimento,* but in its heightened excitement of melodic, rhythmic, and harmonic surprises. The closing section resembles the opening in its eighth-note bass and its repeat of some of the melodic patterns.

The piece is more than a tribute to the composer-pianists of the Romantic age. It is a tribute to an extremely versatile composer with decided gifts for melody, for drama, and for speaking in her own personal idiom to twentieth-century listeners.

List of Works
Orchestral

Chroma—Northern Lights (1986)
Concerto for Piano and Orchestra (1972)
Man's Image and His Cry, for baritone and alto soli, chorus and orchestra (1968)
*Monarchs—*Movement for Large Orchestra (1988)
Sacred Service for the Sabbath Evening, for baritone or alto solo, chorus and orchestra (1976; Galaxy Music)
Tarantelle (Overture for Orchestra) (1985; Galaxy)

Chamber Music

Capriccio, for flute (1971)
Dancer/Inner Dance, for flute, oboe, cello (1985)
De Infinitate Caeleste, for string quartet ("Of the Celestial Infinite") (1980)
Dramatic Fanfare, for brass nonet (1987)
Grand Tarantella, for violin and piano (1970)
Hidden Heritage—A Dance Symphony, for 5 players (flute, clarinet, cello, piano, percussion) (1987)
Music for Two, for any two treble wind, wind/brass instruments (1971; revised version for 2 bass clef instruments, 1985)
Sky Curtains: Borealis, Australis, for flute, B-flat clarinet, bassoon, viola, cello (1984)

Two Movements for Wind Quartet, for flute, oboe, horn, bassoon (1967)
Valse Romantique (1972)
When Angels Speak—Fantasy for Wind Quintet (1987)
Winter Music for Brass Quintet, for 2 trumpets, horn, trombone, tuba
   (1985)

Piano Music

A Calendar Set, 12 virtuosic preludes (1972–78)
Black-Velvet Waltz (1983)
Calendar Collection, 12 preludes for the developing pianist (1976; Alfred
   Publishing)
Nocturne: La Fin de Siècle (1978; Galaxy)
Stone (1981)
2 piano rags: *Reflective Rag, Judy's Rag*

Piano Four-Hands

Snazzy Sonata (1972)
   ''Moderate Two-Step''
   ''Lazy Beguine''
   ''Be-Bop Scherzo''
   ''Valse Brilliante''

Piano Music for Young People

Deceit (1979)
Solitary Pipes (The Joy of Modern Piano Pieces) (1977; Yorktown Music
   Publishing)

Choral Music

The Chase, for chorus, 2 sopranos, alto, tenors, and bass (SSATB), and
   piano, on a text by the composer (1972; Galaxy)
Lamentation, for double chorus, mezzo and baritone soli, piano, and
   percussion, on a text from the old Testament (1982)
Sacred Service for the Sabbath Evening, for baritone or alto solo, chorus,
   piano, (1976; Galaxy)
Serenade: To Music, for chorus and SSATTB, on a text by W. H. Auden
   (1981)
Sunny Airs and Sober Madrigals, for chamber choir and SSATB (1974;
   Walton Music Corp):

"A Questioned Answered" (Shakespeare)
"Winter Mourning" (Shelley)
"Sigh No More, Ladies" (Shakespeare)
"Come Away, Death" (Shakespeare)
"Life Is a Jest" (John Gay, Robert Herrick)

Three Ayres, for chamber choir and SSATB (1969; Broude Brothers):
"O Mistress Mine" (Shakespeare)
"Slow, Slow, Fresh Fount" (Ben Jonson)
"How Sweet I Roam'd" (Blake)

Three Choruses from the Sacred Service, for baritone solo, chorus, SSATB, and piano (or organ) (1976; revised 1980; Galaxy):
"Psalm: The Lord reigneth, let the earth rejoice"
"Why do we deal treacherously, brother against brother?"
"Thou shalt love the Lord"

The Tragical Ballad of Sir Patrick Spens, for chorus, SSATB, choral soli, piano (1980)

Parable: A Tale of Abram and Isaac, dramatic cantata for soprano, tenor, and baritone soli, SATB, chorus, string quintet, and harpsichord (or organ) (1985)

Choral Music for Young People

Moses Supposes, three-part canon for treble voices and percussion (1975; Tetra Music)

Chamber Opera

Goldilocks and the Three Bears (1985)

Solo Voice(s) and Instruments

A Woman of Valor, for mezzo-soprano and string quartet (1977; Transcontinental Music)

From the Great Land: Women's Songs, for mezzo-soprano, clarinet, piano, Eskimo drum, on text by Frank Buske (1982):
"She Is Left on the Ice"
"Passion: The First Dream"
"Lullaby: The Second Dream"
"Counting Song: The Third Dream"
"Lament—Interlude—Lullaby"
"Vision"
"She Dies"

The Magic World: Ritual Music for Three, for baritone, piano, and percussion: wood blocks, tambourine, triangle, cymbals, jingle bells, glocken, tubular bells, tom-tom, bell-tree, glockenspiel; based on Native American texts (1979–80)

Psalm 23, for baritone (or mezzo-soprano), flute, violin, cello, piano (1978; Transcontinental)

Songs of Innocence, for soprano, tenor, flute, cello, harp, on texts by William Blake (1974):
    "Piping Down the Valley Wild"
    "Elegy: The Garden of Love"
    "I Asked a Thief"
    "How Sweet I Roam'd"

Two Songs for Soprano and Harp (1978; Lyra Music Publishing):
    "At Dusk in Summer" (Adrienne Rich)
    "The Ruined Maid" (Thomas Hardy)

Solo Voice and Piano

The Ages of Love, cycle for baritone and piano (1971):
    "The Chaste Love" (Lord Byron)
    "Love's White Heat" (Edna St. Vincent Millay)
    "Disdainful, Fickle Love" (Millay)
    "An Older Love" (Millay)
    "Love's Echo" (Christina Rosetti)

Chansons Nobles et Sentimentales, cycle for high voice and piano (1974):
    "Harmonie du soir" (Baudelaire)
    "Chanson d'automne" (Verlaine)
    "Claire de lune"(Verlaine)
    "Dans l'interminable ennui de la plaine" (Verlaine)
    "Départ" (Rimbaud)

4 songs for mezzo-soprano and piano, on texts by e. e. cummings (1965):
    "Anyone lived in a pretty how town"
    "Three wealthy sisters"
    "The sky"
    "Most people"

Greyed Sonnets: Five Serious Songs, cycle for soprano and piano (1975; Galaxy):
    "Soliloquy" (Millay)
    "Let It Be Forgotten" (S. Teasdale)
    "A Season's Song" (Millay)
    "Love's Autumn" (Millay)
    "Entreaty" (Rosetti)

In the Theater of Night, dream songs on poems of Carl Shapiro, cycle for high voice and piano (1983; Galaxy):

  "Flyers"
  "The Alphabet"
  "A Cut Flower"
  "Calling the Child"
  "Madrigal"
  "Piano"

Nattens Monolog—Night Soliloquy, scena for soprano and piano on text by Dag Hammarskjold (1984)

New-Fashioned Songs, for low voice and piano (1983):

  "Fair Daffodils" (Herrick)
  "When, Dearest" (Suckling)
  "The Eagle" (Tennyson)
  "It Is a Beauteous Evening" (Wordsworth)
  "The Host of the Air" (Yeats)

Discography

A Calendar Set (Twelve Preludes for Solo Piano): Leonarda #101
Chansons Nobles et Sentimentales: Leonarda #101
Greyed Sonnets: Golden Crest 5051
The Magic World: Ritual Music for Three: Leonarda #116
Nocturne: La Fin de Siécle: Leonarda #101
Parables: Leonarda #328
Serenade: Leonarda #328
Songs of Innocence, for soprano, tenor, flute, cello, and harp: Golden Crest 5051
Sunny Airs and Sober, A Book of Madrigals: Golden Crest 5051
Three Ayres: Golden Crest 5051
Two Songs for Soprano and Harp: Leonarda #106

Other Publications

Editor with Karen Famera of *Contemporary Concert Music by Women* (Westport, CT: Greenwood Press, 1981).

Editor, with associate editors Jane Gottlieb and Catherine Overhauser, of *The Musical Woman,* vols. 1 and 2 (Westport, CT: Greenwood Press, 1983, 1987).

"An Annotated List of Twentieth Century Repertoire for the Piano,"
The Piano Teacher's Guidebook (New York: Yorktown Music Press,
1979).

Selected Bibliography

Brookes, Stephen. "Musical Arts' American Blend." *The Washington Post,* March
  21, 1988.
Davis, Peter G. "Piano Still Stirs Composers' Souls." *New York Times,* June 7,
  1981.
Delatiner, Barbara. "Musicians from Hofstra Spread L.I. Word." *The New York
  Times,* March 13, 1988.
Ericson, Raymond. "Soprano: Lucille Field, All-Woman Bill." *New York Times,*
  April 15, 1980.
LePage, Jane Weiner. "Judith Lang Zaimont." In *Women Composers, Conductors,
  and Musicians of the Twentieth Century,* vol. 2. Metuchen, NJ: Scarecrow
  Press, 1983.
The New Grove Dictionary of American Music, ed. H. Wiley Hitchcock and Stanley
  Sadie. S.v. "Zaimont, Judith Lang," by Elizabeth Wood. London and New
  York: Macmillan Press, 1986.
Sparber, Gordon. "Zaimont Wins Guggenheim." *The Peabody News,* Fall, 1984.
White, Stephen. "Orchestra Saves Season's Best for Last." *The Greenville News,*
  April 24, 1988.

To contact Judith Lang Zaimont, write to her concert manager:
Michael Leavitt
Allied Artists' Bureau
170 W. 74th St.
New York, NY 10023
212-874-3990

or contact:
The American Music Center
250 W. 54th St. (Rm. 300)
New York, NY 10019

Appendixes

Appendix 1: Music Appreciation Textbooks Ranked in Order of Number of Women Composers Mentioned

AUTHOR, TITLE, PUBLISHER, DATE, NUMBER OF PAGES	TOTAL NUMBER OF WOMEN COMPOSERS MENTIONED	NUMBER OF MUSIC EXAMPLES COMPOSED BY WOMEN	NUMBER OF COMPLETE PARAGRAPHS DISCUSSING A PARTICULAR WOMAN COMPOSER	NAMES OF COMPOSERS
Levy, Kenneth, *Music: A Listener's Guide* (Harper & Row, 1983), 491	13	0	3	Casia Hildegard of Bingen Clara Schumann Francesca Caccini Barbara Strozzi Elisabeth Jacquet de La Guerre Maria Teresia von Paradis Cécile Chaminade Ethel Smyth Amy Beach Barbara Kolb Thea Musgrave Pauline Oliveros
Kerman, Joseph and Vivian, *Listen* (Worth, 1980), 545	7	0	5	Clara Schumann Fanny Mendelssohn Hensel Barbara Strozzi Beatriz de Dia Gormunda of Montpellier

Reference				Names
				Joni Mitchell Carole King
Politoske, Daniel, *Music*, 3rd ed. (Prentice-Hall, 1984), 450	5	0	0	Esther Williamson Ballou Pozzi Escot Thea Musgrave Clara Schumann Toshiko Akiyoski
Borroff, Edith, and Marjory Ivin, *Music in Perspective* (Harcourt Brace Jovanovich, 1976), 303	4	0	2	Marie de Bourgogne Joan Baez Carole King Germaine Tailleferre
Wingell, Robert, *Experiencing Music* (Alfred, 1981), 453	4*	0	0	Joan Baez Joni Mitchell Judy Collins Janis Joplin
Machlis, Joseph, *The Enjoyment of Music*, 5th ed. (Norton, 1984), 608	3	1	9	Julia Perry Ruth Crawford Thea Musgrave
Manoff, Tom, *Music: A Living Language* (Norton, 1982), 468	2	0	26	Joni Mitchell Karla Bonoff
Hoffer, Charles, *The Understanding of Music* (Wadsworth, 1981), 512	2	0	0	Amy Beach Pauline Oliveros

AUTHOR, TITLE, PUBLISHER, DATE, NUMBER OF PAGES	TOTAL NUMBER OF WOMEN COMPOSERS MENTIONED	NUMBER OF MUSIC EXAMPLES COMPOSED BY WOMEN	NUMBER OF COMPLETE PARAGRAPHS DISCUSSING A PARTICULAR WOMAN COMPOSER	NAMES OF COMPOSERS
Kamien, Roger, *Music: An Appreciation* (McGraw-Hill, 1984), 589	1	0	5	Miriam Gideon
Bamberger, Jeanne, and Howard Brofsky, *Developing Musical Perception* (Harper & Row, 1979), 369	1	0	0	Miriam Gideon
Komar, Arthur, *Music and Human Experience* (Schirmer, 1980), 468	0	0	0	
Byrnside, Robert, *Music, Sound and Sense* (William C. Brown, 1985), 383	0	0	0	

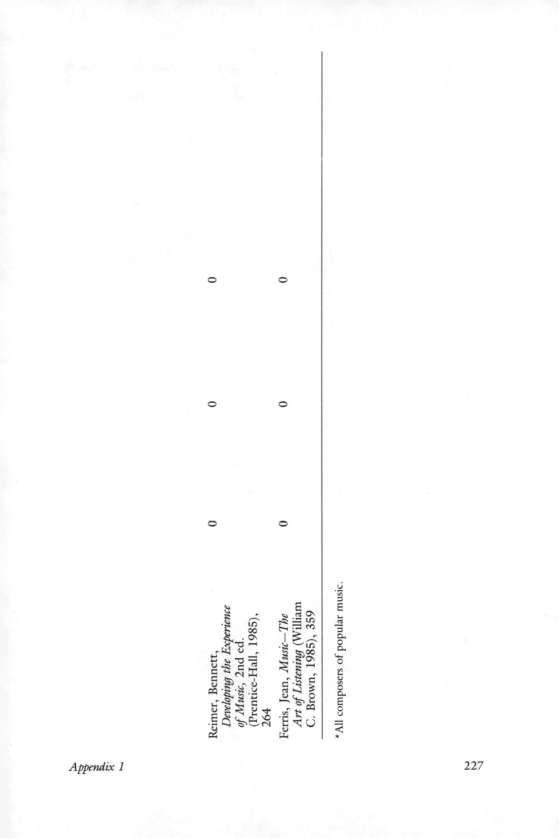

Reimer, Bennett,
*Developing the Experience
of Music,* 2nd ed.
(Prentice-Hall, 1985),
264

Ferris, Jean, *Music—The
Art of Listening* (William
C. Brown, 1985), 359

0   0   0

0   0   0

*All composers of popular music.

Appendix 2: Record Companies Featuring Women Composers

Bridge Record Productions,
 G.P.O.
Box 1864
New York, NY 10023

Cantata
Barenreiter Tonkünstverlag
Barenreiter Weg 6–8
Kassel (35) West Germany

Capriccio Records
7315 Hooking Road
McLean, VA 22101

Composers Recordings, Inc.
 (CRI)
170 W. 74th Street
New York, NY 10023

Desto Records
1860 Broadway
New York, NY 10023

Folkways Records
43 W. 61st Steet
New York, NY 10023

Galaxia Records
P.O. Box 212
Woburn, MA 01801

Genesis
Wayne Stahnke Associates
8244 Tuscanny Avenue
Playa Del Rey, CA 90291

Golden Crest Records
220 Broadway
Huntington Station
New York, NY 11746

Leonarda Productions
P.O. Box 124
Radio City Station
New York, NY 10101

Musical Heritage Society
14 Park Road
Tinton Falls, NJ 07724

New World
Recorded Anthology of
 American Music
231 E. 51st Street
New York, NY 10022

Northeastern Records
P.O. Box 116
Boston, MA 02117

Opus One
P.O. Box 604
Greenville, ME 04441

Orion Master Recordings
Castlerock Road
Malibu, CA 90265

Pelican Records
P.O. Box 32732
Los Angeles, CA 90034

1750 Arch Records
1750 Arch Street
Berkeley, CA 94709

Turnabout
The Moss Music Group
48 W. 38th Street
New York, NY 10018

Appendix 3: An Outline of Western Music from 850 through the 1940s

DATE	SCHOOLS/STYLES	GENRES	MEN COMPOSERS	WOMEN COMPOSERS
850–1100	Romanesque	Plain chants, tropes, sequences	Notker Balbulus (d. 912) Tuotilo (ca. 915) Guido of Arezzo (ca. 997) Wipo (ca. 1000)	
Early Middle Ages 1100–1350	St. Martial School Notre Dame School Provençal troubadours German minnesingers	Organum, discant conductus, laudes, cantigas, motets	Perotin (b.ca. 1155–1160) Leonin (ca. 1163–1190) Adam de la Halle (1237–1284) Franco of Cologne (fl. 1260)	Hildegard von Bingen (1098–1179) Countess Beatrice of Dia (ca. 1140–1212) Maria de Ventadorn (1165–1221) Dame Costelloza (b. 1200)
Late Medieval 1300–1450	French and Italian Sacred and secular Polyphony Burgundian School	Polyphonic ballades, rondeaux, virelais, isorhythmic motets, mass, madrigals, caccia, ballate, Meistersinger songs	G. de Machaut (1300–1377) Jacopo de Bologna (b.ca. 1325) F. Landini (1325–1397)	Christine de Pisan (1363–1431) Marie de Bourgogne (fl. 1450)

DATE	SCHOOLS/STYLES	GENRES	MEN COMPOSERS	WOMEN COMPOSERS
			J. Dunstable (ca. 1380–1453)	
			G. Dufay (ca. 1400–1474)	
			G. Binchois (1400–1460)	
Renaissance 1450–1600	Flemish School Venetian School English madrigals	Frottola, madrigals, masses, motets, instrumental music for ensembles (as well as organ or lute), ricercar, canzona, fantasia, toccata, variations, dance music, early sonatas and suites	J. Ockeghem (1420–1496)	Maddalena Casulana (1540–1583)
			Josquin des Prez (1450–1521)	Tarquinia Molza (1542–1617)
			H. Obrecht (1452–1505)	Raffaela Alcotti (b. 1570)
			J. Arcadelt (ca. 1505–1560)	Vittoria Alcotti (b. 1575)
			G. P. Palestrina (ca. 1526–1594)	
			O. di Lasso (ca. 1532–1594)	
			C. Merulo (1533–1604)	
			T. L. da Victoria (1549–1611)	
			W. Byrd (1543–1623)	
			G. Gabrieli (1554 or 1557–1612)	
			T. Morley (1557–1602)	

Baroque 1600–1750	Nuove musiche: Florentine School Roman School Venetian School Neapolitan School Sacred and secular polyphony (Mature Baroque)	*Vocal:* Monodic style: recitative and basso continuo, opera, oratorio, cantatas *Instrumental:* Chaconne, passacaglia, suite, trio sonata, concerto grosso, fugue, solo sonata	G. Caccini (1546–1618) C. Monteverdi (1567–1643) H. Schütz (1585–1672) S. Landi (1590–1655) J. Chambonnières (ca. 1602–1672) J. Froberger (1616–1672) A. Corelli (1653–1713) A. Scarlatti (1660–1725) A. Vivaldi (1678–1741) J. P. Rameau (1683–1764) J. S. Bach (1685–1750) G. F. Handel (1685–1759)	Francesca Caccini (1587–1640) Isabella Leonarda (1620–1704) Barbara Strozzi (1619–1664) Elisabeth-Claude Jacquet de la Guerre (1666–1729) Antonia Bembo (ca. 1670)

231

DATE	SCHOOLS/STYLES	GENRES	MEN COMPOSERS	WOMEN COMPOSERS
Rococo 1730–1770	Berlin School Mannheim School Gallant Style	Keyboard suites and sonatas, early symphony	K.P.E. Bach (1714–1788) K. P. Stamitz (1717–1757) F. Couperin (1668–1733)	Anna Amalia, Princess of Prussia (1723–1787) Elisabetta de Bambanini (1731–1764)
Classical 1770–1810	Viennese classical style	Opera, concerto, sonata, symphony, string quartet	C. W. Gluck (1714–1787) F.J. Haydn (1732–1809) W. A. Mozart (1756–1791) L. van Beethoven (1770–1827)	Anna Amalia, Duchess of Saxe-Weimar (1739–1807) Marianne Martinez (1744–1812) Corona Schroeter (1751–1802) Maria Theresia von Paradis (1759–1824) Amelie Julie Candeille (1767–1834)

Romantic 1810–1880			
Ideals: Nationalism Individualism Heroism Romantic love Mythology	Songs; character pieces for piano; symphonies; symphonic poems; opera; tone poems; sonatas; ballets; chamber music: trios, quartets, quintets; concerti	G. Rossini (1792–1868) F. P. Schubert (1797–1828) F. Mendelssohn (1809–1847) F. Chopin (1810–1849) R. Schumann (1810–1856) F. Liszt (1811–1886) R. Wagner (1813–1883) G. Verdi (1813–1901) A. Borodin (1833–1887) J. Brahms (1833–1897) G. Bizet (1838–1875) M. Mussorgsky (1839–1881) N. Rimsky-Korsakov (1844–1908) A. Scriabin (1872–1915) S. Rachmaninoff (1873–1943)	Louise Reichardt (1779–1826) Maria Agatha Szymanowska (1789–1831) Louise Farrenc (1804–1875) Fanny Mendelssohn Hensel (1805–1847) Joseph ne Lang (1815–1880) Clara Schumann (1819–1896) Pauline Viardot-Garcia (1821–1910) Ingeborg von Bronsart (1840–1880) Louise Héritte-Viardot (1841–1919) Augusta Mary Holmès (1847–1903) Agathe Backer-Grøndahl (1847–1907) Cécile Chaminade (1857–1944)

DATE	SCHOOLS/STYLES	GENRES	MEN COMPOSERS	WOMEN COMPOSERS
Contemporary Born Before 1900	Impressionism Expressionism Nationalism Folk music Neo–Classicism Serialism Utility music	Conventional and new genres and forms, using new harmonic language	G. Fauré (1845–1924) V. d'Indy (1851–1931) C. Debussy (1862–1918) D. Dukas (1865–1935) G. Holst (1874–1934) A. Schoenberg (1874–1954) C. Ives (1874–1954) M. Ravel (1875–1937) M. de Falla (1876–1946) E. Bloch (1880–1959) B. Bartók (1881–1945)	Ethel Smyth (1858–1944) Amy Beach (1867–1944) Mary Carr Moore (1873–1957) Mabel Daniels (1878–1971) Alma Mahler (1879–1964) Irene Wieniawska Poldowski (1880–1932) Mary Howe (1882–1964) Rebecca Clarke (1886–1979) Florence Price (1888–1953) Marian Bauer (1889–1955) Germaine Tailleferre (1892–1983)

Lili Boulanger (1893–1918)

I. Stravinsky (1882–1971)
A. Webern (1883–1945)
E. Varèse (1883–1965)
A. Berg (1885–1935)
S. Prokofiev (1891–1953)
A. Honegger (1892–1955)
D. Milhaud (1892–1974)
W. Piston (1894–1976)
P. Hindemith (1895–1963)
C. Orff (1895–1982)

A. Copland (b. 1900)
A. Khachaturian (1903–1978)
D. Kabelevsky (1904–1987)
O. Messiaen (b. 1908)
E. Carter (b. 1908)

Ruth Crawford Seeger (1901–1953)
Elizabeth Lutyens (1906–1983)
Miriam Gideon (b. 1906)
Louise Talma (b. 1906)
Peggy Glanville-Hicks (b. 1912)

Music for the films
Electronic music
Aleatoric music
Ballets
Neo-Classicism
Conventional genres

Contemporary Born Between 1900 and 1918

DATE	SCHOOLS/STYLES	GENRES	MEN COMPOSERS	WOMEN COMPOSERS
			J. Cage (b. 1912)	Grazyna Bacewicz (1913–1983)
			B. Britten (1913–1976)	Vivian Fine (b. 1913)
			M. Babbitt (b. 1916)	Julia Smith (b. 1911)
			L. Bernstein (b. 1918)	Margaret Bonds (1913–1972)

Appendix 4: A Selected List of Twentieth-Century Women Composers Born after 1920

COMPOSERS	GENRES
Jean Eichelberger Ivey (b. 1923)	orchestral, chamber, piano, vocal, sacred, film, electronic
Dika Newlin (b. 1923)	orchestral, chamber, piano, electronic, vocal, sacred, opera, popular
Ludmila Ulehla (b. 1923)	orchestral, chamber, flute, vocal
Edith Borroff (b. 1925)	orchestral, chamber, band, piano, vocal, opera, marimba, sacred, organ
Julia Perry (1926–1979)	orchestral, chamber, piano, vocal, sacred, opera
Emma Lou Diemer (b. 1927)	orchestral, band, chamber, organ, piano, vocal, sacred, ballet, opera, electronic
Thea Musgrave (b. 1928)	orchestral, band, chamber, piano, vocal, sacred, ballet, opera, electronic
Ursula Mamlok (b. 1928)	orchestral, chamber, piano, vocal, sacred
Toshiko Akiyoshi (b. 1929)	orchestral, piano, jazz, electronic
Nancy Van de Vate (b. 1930)	orchestral, piano, chamber, vocal, sacred, opera, electronic
Pauline Oliveros (b. 1932)	chamber, piano, vocal, sacred, opera, electronic, multimedia
Alexandra Pierce (b. 1934)	orchestral, chamber, piano, vocal, sacred, theater
Joan Tower (b. 1938)	orchestral, chamber, piano
Meredith Monk (b. 1943)	piano, vocal, opera
Suzanne Ciani (b. 1946)	electronic, film
Laurie Anderson (b. 1947)	electronic, multimedia
Shulamit Ran (b. 1949)	orchestral, chamber, piano, vocal, electronic
Libby Larsen (b. 1950)	chamber, guitar, vocal, sacred, opera
Elizabeth Swados (b. 1950)	orchestral, theater

Appendix 5: A Selected List of Twentieth-Century Women Conductors

Orchestral

Ethel Leginska (1886–1970)
Antonio Brico (b. 1902)
Frederique Petrides (d. 1983)
Dalia Atlas (b. 1935)
Eve Queler (b. 1936)
Catherine Comet (b. 1939)
Rachel Worby (b. 1949)
Victoria Bond (b. 1949)
JoAnn Falletta (b. 1954)
Antonio Joy Wilson (b. 1957)

Choral

Margaret Hillis (b. 1921)

Opera

Sarah Caldwell (b. 1924)
Judith Somogi (1943–1988)
Doris Lang Kosloff (b. 1947)

For Further Reading

Ammer, Christine. *Unsung: A History of Women in American Music.* (Westport, CT: Greenwood Press, 1980).

LePage, Jane Weiner. *Women Composers, Conductors, and Musicians of the Twentieth Century,* vols. 1, 2, and 3 (Metuchen, NJ: Scarecrow Press, 1980, 1983, 1988).

Zaimont, Judith, ed., Jane Gottlieb and Catherine Overhauser, assoc. eds. "Gazette: Conductors." In *The Musical Woman: An International Perspective,* vol. 2 (Westport, CT: Greenwood Press, 1987).

Appendix 6: Recordings Available from Leonarda Productions

Through its critically acclaimed recordings, Leonarda Productions has been at the forefront of the movement to mainstream music by women composers since its founding in 1979. The following list is reprinted from the current Leonarda catalog. Included here are all Leonarda recordings that contain works composed by women. To purchase recordings or to request the complete catalog, write to Leonarda Productions, P.O. Box 1736, Cathedral Station, New York, NY 10025 or telephone (212) 666-7697.

Records
(Cassettes are available where indicated.)

LPI 101, **Judith Lang Zaimont:** *A Calendar Set* (solo piano); *Chansons Noble et Sentimentales* (tenor, piano); *Nocturne* (solo piano). Performed by Gary Steigerwalt; Charles Bressler, Judith Zaimont; Zaimont.

LPI 102, **The New York Bassoon Quartet:** Works by Alvin Brehm, Vaclav Nelhybel, Rudolph Palmer, Peter Schickele, and Katherine Hoover. Performed by Bernadette Zirkuli, Jane Taylor, Lauren Goldstein, Julie Feves.

LPI 103, **Trios for violin, cello, and piano:** Works by Rebecca Clarke and Katherine Hoover. Performed by Suzanne Ornstein, James Kreger, Virginia Eskin; Karen Clarke, Carter Brey, Barbara Weintraub.

LPI 104, **For the Flute:** Louise Farrenc, *Trio in E Minor, Op. 45;* Flute, piano. Lili Boulanger, *Nocturne; D'un Matin de Printemps;* Germaine Tailleferre, *Pastorale;* Katherine Hoover, *On the Betrothal of Princess Isabelle of France, Aged Six Years;* Trio, taped whales: Ludmila Ulehla, *Elegy for a Whale.* Performed by Katherine Hoover, flute; Barbara Weintraub, piano; Carter Brey, cello; Virginia Eskin, piano.

LPI 105, **Music for Flute and Strings by Three Americans:** Amy Beach, *Theme and Variations, Op. 80;* Katherine Hoover, *Divertimento;* Arthur Foote, *A Night Piece.* Performed by Diane Gold; The Alard Quartet.

LPI 106, **Song Cycles for Soprano Plus . . . :** Kurt Weill, *Frauentanz* (singer, flute, clarinet, viola, bassoon, horn); Judith Lang Zaimont, *Two Songs for Soprano and Harp;* Ruth Schonthal, *Totengesänge* (soprano, piano). Performed by Edith Ainsberg, The Bronx Arts Ensemble; Berenice Bramson, Sara Cutler; Bramson, Ruth Schonthal.

LPI 107, **Nineteenth-Century German Lieder:** Fanny Mendelssohn Hensel, Clara Schumann, Pauline Viardot-Garcia, Josephine Lang. Performed by Katherine Ciesinski, mezzo-soprano; John Ostendorf, bass-baritone; Rudolph Palmer, piano.

LIP 109, **French Baroque Cantatas:** Philippe Courbois, Elisabeth Jacquet de la Guerre. Performed by John Ostendorf, bass-baritone; Bronx Arts Ensemble Chamber Orchestra; Johannes Somary, conductor.

LPI 110, **Nineteenth-Century Nonets:** Josef Rheinberger, Louise Farrenc. Performed by the Bronx Arts Ensemble.

LPI 111, **String Quartets:** Lucie Vellère (No. 3), Sarah Aderholdt, Ruth Schonthal, Amy Beach. Performed by the Crescent Quartet: Nancy McAlhany, Alicia Edelberg, Jill Jaffe, Maxine Neuman.

LPI 112 (two discs), **Franz Schubert:** *Die Schöne Müllerin;* **Louise Reichardt:** nine songs; **Fanny Mendelssohn Hensel:** *Six Songs, Op. 1.* Performed by Grayson Hirst, tenor; Michel Yuseph, piano.

LPI 115, **Music for the Mass by Nun Composers:** Hildegard von Bingen, *Kyrie;* Isabella Leonarda, *First Mass, Op. 18.* Performed by Schola Cantorum, University of Arkansas, Fayetteville; Jack Groh, conductor.

LPI 116, **Poems and Magic:** Ned Rorem, *Last Poems of Wallace Stevens* (soprano, cello, piano); Judith Lang Zaimont, *The Magic World* (baritone, piano, percussion). Performed by Rosalind Rees, Sharon Robinson, Jerome Lowenthal; David Arnold, Zita Zohar, Jonathan Haas.

LPI 117, **Karel Husa:** *String Quartet No. 1;* **Priaulx Rainier:** *Quartet for Strings.* Performed by The Alard Quartet.

LPI 118, **Lili Boulanger:** *Clairières dans le Ciel* (soprano, piano); **Alma Mahler:** *Vier Lieder* (mezzo-soprano, piano). Performed by Kristine Ciesinski, Katherine Ciesinski, Ted Taylor.

LPI 119, **On the Edge:** Julie Kabat, five works for pitched or spoken voice, in combination with glass harmonica, violin, piano, African drums, congas, saw, and kalimba. Performed by Julie Kabat, voice, glass harmonica, saw, kalimba; Ben Hudson, violin; Marilyn Crispell, piano; Abraham Adzenyah, African drums and congas.

LPI 120, **Songs of American Composers:** Lee Hoiby, five songs; Ellen Taaffe Zwilich, *Einsame Nacht;* Rebecca Clarke, six songs. Performed by Kristine Ciesinski, soprano; John Ostendorf, bass-baritone; Shirley Seguin, piano; Lee Hoiby, piano.

LPI 121 (LPI 221 for cassette), **Flute Reflections:** Katherine Hoover,

The Medieval Suite (flute, piano), *Reflections* (solo flute); Barbara Kolb, *Homage to Keith Jarrett and Gary Burton* (flute, vibraphone); Elias Tanenbaum, *Transformations* (flute, tape). Performed by Katherine Hoover, Mary Ann Brown, William Moersch.

LPI 122, **Clarinet • Violin • Piano:** Marga Richter, *Landscapes of the Mind II* (violin, piano), *Sonora* (two clarinets, piano); Thomas Christian David, *Duo* (violin, clarinet); Don Freund, *Triomusic* (violin, clarinet, piano). Performed by Daniel Heifetz, Michael Skelly; Stanley and Naomi Drucker, Blanche Abram; The Verdehr Trio: Walter and Elsa Ludewig-Verdehr, Gary Kirkpatrick.

LPI 123, **La Musica:** Sixteenth- and seventeenth-century music by Francesca and Settimia Caccini, Fabritio Caroso, Barbara Strozzi, Sigismondo d'India, Giovanni Kapsberger, Alessandro Piccinni, Francesca Campana, and two unknown composers. Performed by Carol Platamura, soprano; Jürgen Hübscher, lute and baroque guitar; Beverly Lauridsen, viola da gamba.

Cassettes

LPI 1–2 (two cassettes), The **Leonarda Sampler Cassettes,** will introduce you to the composers and artists of Leonarda's twenty-four LP releases through music, voiceover introductions, and words from composers themselves, including interviews with eleven of Leonarda's women composers.

LPI 3–4 (two cassettes), **Women Composers: The Lost Tradition Found,** provides the thirty-eight musical examples discussed in this book.

Compact Discs

LE 325, **Collage:** Carl Czerny, *Fantasia, Op. 256* (flute, cello, piano); Eugene Goossens, *Five Impressions of a Holiday* (flute, cello, piano); Arthur Foote, *Three Pieces* (flute, oboe, cello); Katherine Hoover, *Lyric Trio* (flute, cello, piano); Gustav Holst, *Terzetto* (flute, oboe, cello); Thea Musgrave, *Impromptu No. 1* (flute, oboe). Performed by The Huntingdon Trio: Diane Gold, flute; Lloyd Smith, cello; Rheta Smith, piano and oboe.

LE 326, **The Verdehr Trio: Trios for Violin, Clarinet, and Piano:** Max Bruch, *Four Pieces* from Op. 83; Leslie Bassett, *Trio;* Charles Hoag, *Inventions on the Summer Solstice;* Katherine Hoover, *Images.*

LE 327, **Journeys: Orchestral Works by American Women:** Nancy

Van de Vate, *Journeys;* Kay Gardner; *Rainforest;* Libby Larsen, *Overture—Parachute Dancing;* Marga Richter, *Lament;* Katherine Hoover, *Summer Night* (soloists: Katherine Hoover, flute; Peter Kane, horn); Ursula Mamlok, *Elegy;* Jane Brockman, *Perihelion II.* First six pieces performed by the Bournemouth Sinfonietta, augmented by twenty-five players for the Van de Vate and Larsen works. The seventh piece performed by the Arioso Chamber Orchestra. Conducted by Carolann Martin.

Selected Bibliography

General Interest

Borroff, Edith. "Women Composers: Reminiscence and History." *College Music Symposium, Journal of the College Music Society,* 15 (Spring 1975).

Drinker, Sophie. *Women and Music.* New York: Coward-McCann, 1977. (Reprint of 1948 ed. by Longmans, Green & Co., Toronto.)

Elson, Arthur. *Women's Work in Music.* Portland, ME: Longwood Press, 1976. (Reprint of the 1904 ed.).

Upton, George Putnam. *Women in Music,* 6th ed. Chicago: McClury Press, 1899.

Zaimont, Judith, ed., Jane Gottlieb and Catherine Overhauser, assoc. eds. *The Musical Woman: An International Perspective,* vol. 1 and 2. Westport, CT: Greenwood Press, 1983, 1987. Articles on music criticism, music business (including arts administration, patrons, the recording industry), festivals, concert series and conferences, music education, electronic composers, and specific composers.

Historical

Bogin, Meg. *The Women Troubadours.* New York: Norton, 1978.

Bowers, Jane, and Judith Tick, eds. *Women Making Music: The Western Art Tradition, 1150–1950.* Urbana, IL: University of Illinois Press, 1986.

Neuls-Bates, Carol, ed. *Women in Music: An Anthology of Source Readings from the Middle Ages to the Present.* New York: Harper & Row, 1982.

U.S. Women Composers

Ammer, Christine. *Unsung: A History of Women in American Music.* Westport, CT: Greenwood Press, 1980.

Block, Adrienne Fried, and Carol Neuls-Bates. *Women in American Music: Bibliography of Music and Literature.* Westport, CT: Greenwood Press, 1979.

Skowronski, JoAnn. *Women in American Music: A Bibliography.* Metuchen, NJ: Scarecrow Press, 1978

Smith, Julia, comp. *Directory of American Women Composers.* Chicago: National Federation of Music Clubs, 1970.

Tick, Judith. *American Women Composers Before 1879.* Ann Arbor, MI: UMI Press, 1983.

Black Women Composers

Green, Mildred Denby. *Black Women Composers: A Genesis.* Boston: Twayne, 1983.

Southern, Eileen. *The Music of Black Americans.* New York: Norton, 1971.

Specific Genres

Claghorn, Gene. *Women Composers and Hymnists: A Biographical Dictionary.* Metuchen, NJ: Scarecrow Press, 1984.

MacAuslan, Janna. *A Catalog of Compositions for Guitar by Women Composers.* Portland, OR: Dear Horse Publications, 1984.

Meggett, Joan M. *Keyboard Music by Women Composers, A Catalog and Bibliography.* Westport, CT: Greenwood Press, 1981.

Rogal, Samuel. *Sisters of Sacred Song: A Selected Listing of Women Hymnodists in Great Britain and America.* New York: Garland Publishing, 1981.

Stewart-Green, Miriam. *Women Composers: A Checklist for the Solo Voice.* Boston: G. K. Hall, 1980.

Twentieth-Century Women Composers

Anderson, Ruth, ed. *Contemporary American Composers, A Biographical Dictionary.* Boston: G. K. Hall, 1982.

Hixon, Donald L. *Thea Musgrave: A Bio-Bibliography.* Westport, CT: Greenwood Press, 1984.

LePage, Jane Weiner, ed. *Women Composers, Conductors, and Musicians of the Twentieth Century: Selected Biographies,* vol. 1, 2, 3. Metuchen, NJ: Scarecrow Press, 1980, 1983, 1988.

Monson, Karen. *Alma Mahler. Muse to Genius.* Boston: Houghton Mifflin, 1983.

Rosen, Judith. *Grazyna Bacewicz: Her Life and Works.* Los Angeles: Friends of Polish Music, University of Southern California School of Music, 1984.

Wood, Elizabeth. *Banners and Music: The Life of Ethel Smyth*. London: Jonathan Cape, forthcoming.

Zaimont, Judith, and Karen Famera, eds. *Contemporary Concert Music by Women: A Directory of the Composers and Their Works*. Westport, CT: Greenwood Press, 1981.

Women Composers and Performers of Popular Genres

Dahl, Linda. *Stormy Weather: The Music and Lives of a Century of Jazzwomen*. New York: Pantheon Books, 1984.

Handy, Antoinette. *The International Sweethearts of Rhythm*. Metuchen, NJ: Scarecrow Press, 1983.

Leder, Jan. *Women in Jazz: A Discography of Instrumental Music, 1913–1968*. Westport, CT: Greenwood Press, 1985.

McManus, Jill. "Women Jazz Composers and Arrangers." In *The Musical Woman*, vol. 2, ed. Judith Zaimont. Westport, CT: Greenwood Press, 1987.

Placksin, Sally. *American Women in Jazz*. New York: Wideview, 1982.

Stewart-Baxter, Derrick. *Ma Rainey and the Classic Blues Singers*. New York: Stein & Day, 1970.

Unterbrink, Mary. *Jazzwomen at the Keyboard*. Jefferson, NC: MacFarland Press, 1983.

Women and Folk Music: A Select Bibliography. Washington, D.C.: Archive of Folk Song, Library of Congress, 1978.

Reference

Cohen, Aaron. *International Encyclopedia of Women Composers*. 2d rev. ed. 2 vols. New York: Books and Music, 1987.

Hixon, Donald, and Donald Hennessee, comps. *Women in Music: A Bibliography*. Metuchen, NJ: Scarecrow Press, 1975.

Pool, Jean. *Handbook: Teaching the History of Women in Music*. Northridge, CA: California State University, Department of Music, 1986.

Stern, Susan. *Women Composers: A Handbook*. Metuchen, NJ: Scarecrow Press, 1978.

Musical Scores: Series

Arsis Press/Sisra Publications, Washington, D.C. Solo vocal and instrumental music, vocal and instrumental chamber music, sacred choral music, totaling over seventy works by Judith Shatin Allen, Mary van Appledorn, Lyle de Bohun, Harriet Bolz, Jane Brockman, Ann Callaway, Emma Lou Diemer, Bertha Terry Donahue, Vivian Fine, Jane Frasier, Winifred Hyson, Anna Larson, Ruth Lomon, Frances Thompson McKay, Alexandra Pierce, Ruth Schonthal, Clare Shore, Nancy Van de Vate, Elizabeth Vercoe, Gwyneth Walker, and Vally Weigl.

Nine Centuries of Music by Women, Williamstown, MA: Broude Brothers.
Choral music:

1. Francesca Caccini, *Aure volanti* for SSA, 3 flutes and continuo
2. Barbara Strozzi, *Consiglio amoroso* for SAB and continuo
3. Barbara Strozzi, *Con le belle non ci vuol fretta* for SATB and continuo
4. Elisabeth Jacquet de la Guerre, *Raccommodement comique de Pierrot et de Nicole* for S, baritone soloist, chorus and continuo
5–10. Louise Reichardt, *Sechs geistliche Lieder* for SSAA, and piano; Set A, 3 songs, nos. 5–7; Set B, 3 songs, nos. 8–10.
11. Isabella Leonarda, *Ave Regina Caelorum* for S,A,T solo, SATB and continuo
12. Raffaella Aleotti, *Ascendens Christus in altum* for SATTB
13. Raffaella Aleotti, *Facta est cum Angelo* for SAATB
14. Vittoria Aleotti, *Baciai per haver vita* for SATB
15. Vittoria Aleotti, *Hor che la vaga Aurora* for SATB

Women Composer Series. Jersey City, NJ: Da Capo Press. Piano solo, vocal, and instrumental music:

1. Amy Beach, *Quintet for Piano and Strings in F# Minor,* op. 67
2. Cécile Chaminade, *Three Piano Works: Piano Sonata in C Minor,* op. 21, *Etude Symphonique,* op. 28, *Six Concert Etudes,* op. 35.
3. Louise Farrenc, *Trio in E Minor for Piano, Flute, and Cello,* op. 45.
4. Clara Schumann, *Selected Piano Music*
5. Rebecca Clarke, *Trio for Piano, Violin, and Cello* (1921)
6. Fanny Hensel, *Trio for Piano, Violin and Cello in D Minor,* op. 11
7. Louise Reichardt, *Songs*
8. Ethel Smyth, *Mass in D*
9. Agathe Bäcker Grøndahl, *Piano Music*
10. Amy Beach, *Piano Music*
11. Josephine Lang, *Songs*
12. Mary Carr Moore, *David Rizzio*
13. Augustra Holmès, *Selected Songs*
14. Maria Malibran, *Album lyrique et dernières pensées*
15. Teresa Carreño, *Piano Music*
16. Nadia Boulanger, *Songs*
17. Cécile Chaminade, *Album of Songs,* Vol. I
18. Marion Bauer, *Sonata for Violin and Piano*
19. Amy Beach, *Sonata for Violin and Piano,* op. 34
20. Rebecca Clarke, *Sonata for Viola and Piano*
21. Barbara Strozzi, *Sacri Musicali Affeti,* op. 5
22. Louise Puget and Jane Vieu, *Anthology of Songs*
23. Franziska Lebrun, *Keyboard Sonatas*
24. Mary Carr Moore, *28 Songs*
25. Amy Beach, *23 Songs*

Musical Scores: Anthologies

Belisle, John, ed. *American Artsong Anthology,* vol. 1, *Contemporary American Songs for High Voice and Piano.* New York: Galaxy Music, 1982. Songs by Miriam Gideon, Jean E. Ivey, and Judith Zaimont.

Briscoe, James, ed. *Historical Anthology of Music by Women*. Bloomington: Indiana University Press, 1987. Vocal and instrumental music from the Middle Ages to the present by Kassia, Hildegard von Bingen, Countess of Dia, Anne Boleyn, Maddalena Casulana, Francesca Caccini, Isabella Leonarda, Elizabeth-Claude Jacquet de la Guerre, Maria Margherita Grimani, Anna Amalie, Marianne von Martinez, Maria Theresia von Paradis, Maria Szymanowska, Josephine Lang, Fanny Mendelssohn Hensel, Clara Schumann, Louise Farrenc, Pauline Viardot-Garcia, Amy Beach, Cécile Chaminade, Dame Ethel Smyth, Lili Boulanger, Alma Mahler, Rebecca Clarke, Germaine Tailleferre, Ruth Crawford Seeger, Miriam Gideon, Grazyna Bacewicz, Louise Talma, Julia Perry, Vivian Fine, Violet Archer, Pauline Oliveros, Thea Musgrave, and Ellen Taaffe Zwilich.

Drucker, Ruth and Helen Strine, eds. *A Collection of Art Songs by Women Composers*. Fulton, MD: HERS Publishing, 1988. Includes Louise Reichardt, Isabella Colbran, Fanny Mendelssohn Hensel, Poldowski (Irene Wieniawska), Lili Boulanger, Marguerite Canal, Amy Beach, Eleanor Freer, Marion Bauer, and Carrie Jacobs Bond.

Lindeman, Carolyn, comp. *Women Composers of Ragtime*. Bryn Mawr, PA: Theodore Presser, 1985. Rags by Adaline Shepher, Julia Lee Niebergall, Irene Giblin, and May Aufderheide.

Patterson, Willis, comp. *Anthology of Art Songs by Black Composers*. Melville, NY: Belwin Mills, 1977. Songs by Margaret Bonds, Undine Smith Moore, and Florence Price.

Rieder, Eva and Kaete Walter, eds. *Female Composers: 22 Piano Pieces*. Mainz, West Germany: B. Schott Söhne, 1985. Includes Fanny Mendelssohn Hensel, Cecile Chaminade, Lili Boulanger, Elisabeth Lutyens, and others.

Discographies

Cohen, Aaron. *International Discography of Women Composers*. Westport, CT: Greenwood Press, 1984.

Frasier, Jane. *Women Composers, a Discography*. Detroit: Information Coordinators (Detroit Studies in Music Bibliography), 1983.

Acknowledgments

The English translations of the texts of the following works are copyright © by Leonarda Productions and are reprinted by permission. The names of the translators are given in parentheses.

Francesca Caccini, *Chi desia si saper', che cos' è amore* (Carol Plantamura)
Barbara Strozzi, *Tradimento!* (Carol Plantamura)
Elisabeth-Claude Jacquet de la Guerre, *Tempête* from *Le Sommeil d'Ulisse* (John Ostendorf)
Louise Reichardt, *Heir liegt ein Spielmann begraben* and *Bettley der Vögel* (Grayson Hirst)
Fanny Mendelssohn Hensel, *Nachtwanderer* (John Ostendorf); *Warum sind denn die Rosen so blass* and *Morgenständchen* (Grayson Hirst)
Josephine Lang, *Der Winter, Frühzeitiger Frühling,* and *Wie glänzt so hell dein Auge* (John Ostendorf)
Clara Weick Schumann, *Das ist ein Tag der klingen mag, Warum willst du and're fragen?, Er ist gekommen in Sturm und Regen,* and *Liebst du um Schönheit* (John Ostendorf)
Pauline Viardot-Garcia, *Das Vöglein* and *Die Beschwörung* (John Ostendorf)

Quotations from the jacket notes from *Music for Flute and Strings by Three Americans* (LPI 105), *Songs of American Composers* (LPI 120), *The Crescent Quartet* (LPI 111), and *Clarinet, Violin, Piano* (LPI 122) are copyright © by Leonarda Productions and are reprinted by permission.

"Destiny" and "Elizabeth," from *Poems* by Herman Hesse, selected and translated by James Wright, copyright © 1970 by James Wright, are reprinted by permission of Farrar, Strauss and Giroux, Inc.

Quotations from the correspondence of September 17, 1986 from Ruth Schonthal to Diane Jezic are included here with the permission of Ruth Schonthal.

Quotations from Barbara Kolb's program notes to *Homage to Keith Jarrett and Gary Burton* are from the score published by Boosey and Hawkes, Inc., and are reprinted with permission.

"Music Appreciation Texts Ranked in Order of Number of Composers Mentioned" by Diane Jezic is from "A Survey of College Music Textbooks: Benign Neglect of Women Composers?" by Diane Jezic and Daniel Binder, in *The Musical Woman: An International Perspective*, vol. 2, 1984–1985, Judith Lang Zaimont, Editor-in-Chief (Greenwood Press, Inc., Westport, CT, 1987), pp. 448–50 (or 451). Copyright © by Judith Lang Zaimont. Reprinted with permission of the publisher and Daniel Binder.

The Feminist Press at The City University of New York offers alternatives in education and in literature. Founded in 1970, this nonprofit, tax-exempt educational and publishing organization works to eliminate sexual stereotypes in books and schools and to provide literature with a broad vision of human potential. The publishing program includes reprints of important works by women, feminist biographies of women, and nonsexist children's books. Curricular materials, bibliographies, directories, and a quarterly journal provide information and support for students and teachers of women's studies. In-service projects help to transform teaching methods and curricula. Through publications and projects, The Feminist Press contributes to the rediscovery of the history of women and the emergence of a more humane society.

New and Forthcoming Books

Black Foremothers: Three Lives, 2nd ed., by Dorothy Sterling. Foreword by Margaret Walker. Introduction by Barbara Christian. $9.95 paper.

Get Smart: A Woman's Guide to Equality on Campus, by Montana Katz and Veronica Vieland. $29.95 cloth, $9.95 paper.

Islanders, a novel by Helen R. Hull. Afterword by Patricia McClelland Miller. $10.95 paper.

Library and Information Sources on Women: A Guide to Collections in the Greater New York Area, compiled by the Women's Resources Group of the Greater New York Metropolitan Area Chapter of the Association of College and Research Libraries and the Center for the Study of Women and Society of the Graduate School and University Center of The City University of New York. $12.95 paper.

Lone Voyagers: Academic Women in Coeducational Universities, 1869–1937, edited by Geraldine J. Clifford. $29.95 cloth, $12.95 paper.

My Mother Gets Married, a novel by Moa Martinson. Translated and introduced by Margaret S. Lacy. $8.95 paper.

Not So Quiet: Stepdaughters of War, a novel by Helen Zenna Smith. Afterword by Jane Marcus. $9.95 paper.

Ruth Weisburg: Paintings, Drawings, Prints, 1968–1988, edited and curated by Marion E. Jackson. With an essay by Thalia Gouma-Peterson. $15.00 paper.

Sultana's Dream and Selections from The Secluded Ones, by Rokeya Sakhawat Hossain. Edited and translated by Roushan Jahan. Afterword by Hanna Papanek. $16.95 cloth, $6.95 paper.

We That Were Young, a novel by Irene Rathbone. Introduction by Lynn Knight. Afterword by Jane Marcus. $10.95 paper.

Women Activists: Challenging the Abuse of Power, by Anne Witte Garland. Foreword by Ralph Nader. Introduction by Frances T. Farenthold. $29.95 cloth, $9.95 paper.

For a free catalog, write to The Feminist Press at The City University of New York, 311 East 94 Street, New York, NY 10128. Send individual book orders to The Talman Company, Inc., 150 Fifth Avenue, New York, NY 10011. Please include $1.75 for postage and handling for one book, $.75 for each additional.